FURNITURE-MAKING TECHNIQUES FOR THE WOOD CRAFTSMAN

FURNITURE-MAKING TECHNIQUES FOR THE WOOD CRAFTSMAN

GUILD OF MASTER CRAFTSMAN PUBLICATIONS LTD

This collection first published 1999 by

Guild of Master Craftsman Publications Ltd,
Castle Place, 166 High Street, Lewes,
East Sussex BN7 IXU

Front cover photographs, left to right, top to bottom:
Stephen Hepworth, Bill Cain, Anthony Bailey
Anthony Bailey, Bob Wearing
Chris Skarbon, Bob Wearing

Back cover photographs: Manny Cefai (top), Tim Judson (bottom)

Article photography by: Anthony Bailey (pp. 2-5, 24-5, 53, 70-2, 74-6),
Dennis Bunn (p. 73), Manny Cefai (pp. 58-61),
Stephen Hepworth (pp. 77-80), Sandor Nagyszalnczy (pp. 12-15),
Paul Richardson (p. 6), Chris Skarbon (p. 85)

Other photographs by the authors.

Illustrations by Simon Rodway except:
Bob Wearing (pp. 37-9, 42-5), Andrew Skelton (p. 83)

Designed by Edward Le Froy and Jenni Keeble

Printed and bound by Kyodo Printing (Singapore) under the supervision of
MRM Graphics, Winslow, Buckinghamshire, UK

CONTENTS

NOTE

Every effort has been made to ensure that the information in this book
is accurate at the time of writing but inevitably prices, specifications,
and availability of tools will change from time to time. Readers are
therefore urged to contact manufacturers or suppliers for up-to-date
information before ordering tools.

MEASUREMENTS

Throughout the book instances may be found where a metric measurement
has fractionally varying imperial equivalents, usually within $\frac{1}{16}$in either
way. This is because in each particular case the closest imperial
equivalent has been given.
A mixture of metric and imperial measurements should NEVER be used
– always use either one or the other.

See also detailed metric/imperial conversion charts on page 117.

INTRODUCTION

FURNITURE-MAKING IS, with little doubt, the most demanding of the craft disciplines – none other requires such a breadth of knowledge, diversity of equipment, or range of techniques. While textbooks provide a useful reference for those on the learning curve, traditionally the real secrets and tricks of the trade have been passed on from one craftsman to another in the workshop. This can place the solitary furniture-maker, whether amateur or professional, at a disadvantage.

Happily makers are generous in passing on the benefit of their hard-won experience, and never more so than in the pages of *Furniture & Cabinetmaking* magazine, from which this compilation is drawn, in recognition of the lasting value of the advice and information it contains.

In these pages you will find subjects as varied as making, caring for and using hand tools; the sophisticated manipulation of wood in order to change its shape from curved to straight and vice versa; the servicing and use of machinery; and the mysteries of hand-finishing.

There is little variation, however, in the expertise and authority of the authors; all are established craftsmen, and most are professional furniture-makers who have gained their experience at the bench – in the real world of cabinetmaking. Thus the reader can be confident that these articles are uncluttered by unproven theories, outdated techniques or impractical approaches, and represent as valid a source of information as can be found outside the workshop.

Paul Richardson
Managing Editor (Magazines)

Get to the point

However good your table saw is, its cut is only as good as the blade fitted.
Editor **Paul Richardson** chooses the right one for the job

'VE SAID IT BEFORE in F&C; a good table saw is the
heart of a cabinetmaker's workshop. It can rip down
rough-sawn timber, crosscut prepared stock,
dimension veneered boards and even cut joints –
but to realise its potential in these different
areas the right blade must be fitted.

Condition of the blade is just as
important. Blunt, chipped or
missing teeth, a warped
plate, or even resin build-
up, will drastically
reduce the accuracy
and effective
cutting power
of your saw.

Carbide-tipped tooth

Gullet

Shoulder

Arbor hole
must be
reamed for
true running

This mark indicates
that the blade has
been roller-tensioned

WAVEFORM®
sawblades

TRIMMING / CROSSCUT
FINE FINISH

Order Ref.
TR/250x60x30

PROTECTION
MUST BE WORN

30mm

$\varnothing$ = 250

= 60

MAX
RPM = 7600

QUALITY
CARBIDE BLADE

***trend*®**
sawing technology

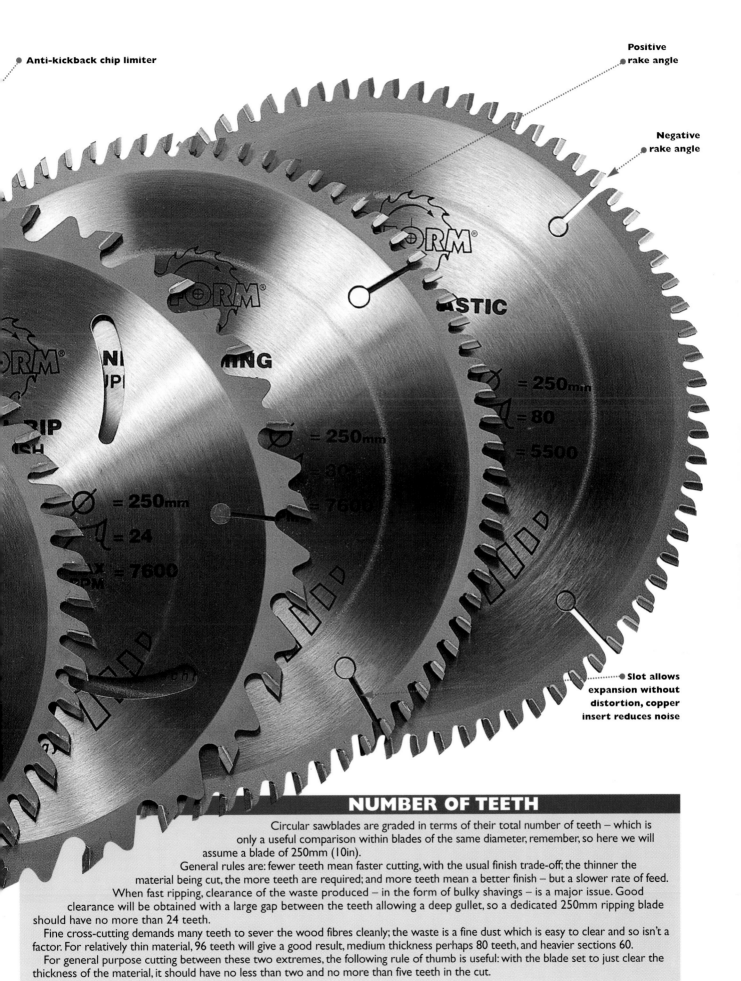

Anti-kickback chip limiter

Positive rake angle

Negative rake angle

Ø = 250mm

= 80

= 5500

Ø = 250mm

= 24

PM = 7600

Slot allows expansion without distortion, copper insert reduces noise

NUMBER OF TEETH

Circular sawblades are graded in terms of their total number of teeth – which is only a useful comparison within blades of the same diameter, remember, so here we will assume a blade of 250mm (10in).

General rules are: fewer teeth mean faster cutting, with the usual finish trade-off; the thinner the material being cut, the more teeth are required; and more teeth mean a better finish – but a slower rate of feed.

When fast ripping, clearance of the waste produced – in the form of bulky shavings – is a major issue. Good clearance will be obtained with a large gap between the teeth allowing a deep gullet, so a dedicated 250mm ripping blade should have no more than 24 teeth.

Fine cross-cutting demands many teeth to sever the wood fibres cleanly; the waste is a fine dust which is easy to clear and so isn't a factor. For relatively thin material, 96 teeth will give a good result, medium thickness perhaps 80 teeth, and heavier sections 60.

For general purpose cutting between these two extremes, the following rule of thumb is useful: with the blade set to just clear the thickness of the material, it should have no less than two and no more than five teeth in the cut.

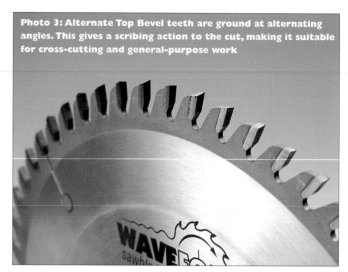

Photo 2: Flat top, or Raker, teeth are ground flat across their tops. This gives good waste clearance when combined with a large gullet and is best for fast ripping

Photo 3: Alternate Top Bevel teeth are ground at alternating angles. This gives a scribing action to the cut, making it suitable for cross-cutting and general-purpose work

Types

Over the last few years Tungsten Carbide Tipped (TCT) blades have come to dominate the market due to their greater working life between sharpenings, so we will ignore the superseded High Speed Steel (HSS) type; these are only needed for specialist applications where their much thinner kerf and greater initial sharpness outweigh their disadvantages. The following comments, therefore, apply only to TCT blades.

FT – Flat Top, or raker – blades have their teeth ground square across the top giving a chisel shape to each tooth, *see photo 2*. This pattern, with its chopping rather than slicing action, gives good waste clearance and fast cutting with the grain, making it the most suitable for ripping; used for cross-cutting it will produce a poor finish and severe tearout.

ATB – Alternate Top Bevel – blades have their teeth ground at alternate bevel angles, *see photo 3*. This gives a slicing action to both sides of the blade, making it the most suitable for cross-cutting; used for ripping it will produce a good finish, although

requiring a much slower feed rate than an FT blade.

ATB blades with extreme bevel angles, *see photo 4*, are available for clean cutting of veneers, delicate laminates and melamine-faced boards. These can produce a superb finish and are especially good for mitring, but will wear quickly.

Combination blades are available which feature both the ATB and FT tooth pattern, intended to give a good finish together with fast waste clearance. In practise they don't perform appreciably better than an ATB blade with a modest bevel angle; however, they will leave a flat-bottomed kerf when used for grooving.

Triple Chip blades have teeth which are ground in two alternate patterns: the first is an FT grind with chamfered corners, the second a lower-profile FT grind, *see photo 5*. The chamfered tooth cuts the centre of the kerf, while the following raker tooth cuts the sides. The purpose of this pattern is to minimise tearout, especially on melamine-faced board. Generally produced with a

shallow, zero or even negative rake angle, they resist wear from abrasive materials such as MDF.

All the angles

The Rake Angle is the angle at which the face of each tooth is ground, measured against the radius of the blade, *see main photo*. As a general rule, the greater the rake angle, the faster and rougher the cut; thus a deep ripping blade might have a rake of 18° to 20°, a general purpose blade around 15°, a good cross-cut blade about 10° and a blade for melamine-faced board from 5° to -7°.

For radial arm and snip-off saws, a negative rake is also a safety feature, as it reduces the tendency for blades to climb up the workpiece.

The Side Clearance Angle is the angle at which the side of each tooth is ground, measured against the radius of the blade. As a general rule, the shallower the clearance angle, the finer the finish; they also mean more friction and therefore heat, though, so are only worth using on end-grain and where finish is critical.

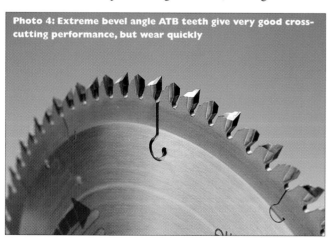

Photo 4: Extreme bevel angle ATB teeth give very good cross-cutting performance, but wear quickly

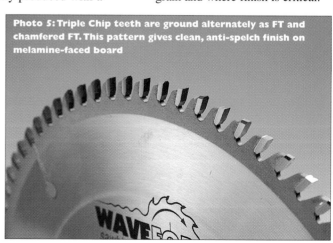

Photo 5: Triple Chip teeth are ground alternately as FT and chamfered FT. This pattern gives clean, anti-spelch finish on melamine-faced board

The hump behind each tooth seen on some rip blades, *see photo*, is not a fashion statement, but a chip limiter; its purpose is to restrict the amount of cut. This not only saves wear and heat build-up, but reduces the risk of kickback from a blade jammed in the cut.

The wiggly lines now so modish are intended to reduce noise.

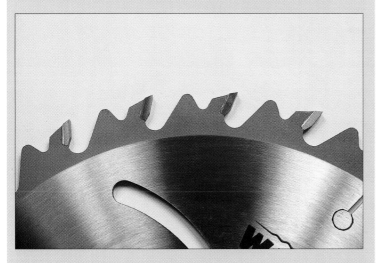

Kerf width

The typical kerf width of a TCT sawblade is between 3.5 and 4.0mm; blades with a narrow kerf of as little as 2.0mm (small diameter blades only) to 2.8mm are available. The advantages of a narrow kerf are: less power required to drive the blade, therefore improved performance from small machines; and less waste is produced – important when cutting valuable exotics.

Drawbacks are faster wear and a greater risk of heat build-up, the latter sometimes leading to distortion of the blade's plate – which is also thinner than that of a standard blade.

Quality

Sawblade quality starts with the plate itself – however well the teeth are ground, if they're wobbling about on the edge of a buckled plate the cut will be unsatisfactory. Good plates are roller-tensioned – visible as a faint ring on the plate at about three-quarters of its diameter – and almost dead flat. The latter may be checked with the blade of an engineer's square.

The second most important factor is the quality of tooth-grinding. This is less easily checked, although a good magnifying glass will reveal the grinding marks if compared with a known poor example. While peering at the tooth-grind, make a visual check of the brazing – this should be smooth and free of fissures and pinholes; lumpy brazing is a bad sign.

Carbide quality is hard to check – if the manufacturer describes it as 'micrograin' and is prepared to quote a grade number, you should be reassured.

The arbor hole is often overlooked, but is a vital element as a misaligned, oversized or eccentric hole will ruin a blade's performance. Good holes are reamed to exact size, a process that leaves a smooth, burnished finish. Avoid blades with sharp, burred holes, and any indication that the hole has been punched out is cause for instant rejection.

Price is a partial indicator of quality – you do get what you pay for, most of the time. This is not to say that bargains can't be had, or that money can't be wasted!

Recommendation

So from the thousands of blades on offer, what should a furniture-maker choose? Specialists in, say, MDF furniture, or those who use a lot of large-section hardwoods, will have special requirements, but for the average bloke at the bench – like myself – it is easier to suggest a basic requirement – again, assuming a 250mm (10in) machine.

As a general purpose workhorse, a 40 to 48 tooth ATB blade with a 5 or 10° bevel will cope with most work, so buy one of these first and add the following as they are needed: if you use a reasonable amount of hardwood bought rough-sawn, a 24 tooth FT ripping blade will prove useful; for fine cross-cutting, joint-cutting and board work, keep an 80 tooth ATB blade with a 10 or 15° bevel nice and sharp; and if your work includes melamine-faced board, then the clean cut and wear-resistance of an 80 tooth, negative rake, triple chip blade will make life easier for you.

Remember, it is better to have a limited range of good quality blades than a stack of cheap ones. ■

We acknowledge the assistance given by Trend in preparing this article. Contact them at: **Trend Machinery & Cutting Tools Ltd**, Unit 6, Odhams Trading Estate, Watford, Herts. WD2 5TR (tel: 01923 249911, fax: 01923 236879)

Violin maker **Dominic Excell** explains
how he sharpens his edge tools

Sharpening edge tools

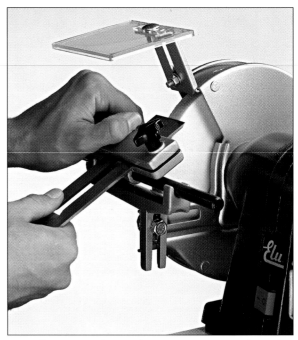

ABOVE: A bench grinder with a good tool-clamp is needed.

I N MY MANY years of making violins and teaching others how to make them, it has been proved time and again how much easier it is to achieve the desired results when razor-sharp tools are used.

Everyone has their own method of sharpening, of course, but that described here works extremely well on all edge tools for use in work of a fairly light nature; it allows for accurate cutting and absolute control with light pressure.

Chisels

I will start with the sharpening of chisel blades.

The essential principle of this method is that after the front face of the blade is hollow ground, final sharpening is carried out with oil or water stones bridging over the hollow grinding, thus ensuring the bevel angle is flat and not rounded over.

This method doesn't take long to master. I don't recommend a honing guide, by the way, as I feel that a considerable degree of control is forfeited. The only mechanical requirement is a 125mm, 5in diameter grinding wheel, ideally with a clamping device to enable the tool to be slid from side to side while being held at the correct angle.

Honing

The back of the blade must be well polished without rounding over at the edge. I cannot emphasise too strongly how important this last point is. Once you have the back

honed to eliminate machining marks, scratches etc, use only the finest grade upon it unless deep scratches occur from misuse!

I use Japanese water stones for honing, as an extremely sharp edge can be obtained while eliminating the danger of dirt-attracting oily deposits which can result from the use of oil stones. Honing guides should never be used on water stones as they will quickly wear the surface.

The fine stone is used after a few strokes with a medium variety to remove grinding marks on the bevelled side. A leather strop can be used for a final polish, but here again great care must be used, as it is all too easy to round over the edge!

Plane irons

Disregard the sharpening instructions that come with a new plane, unless heavy duty work is to be undertaken.

The shape of a plane iron's cutting edge as well as its profile is important. For the task of jointing boards accurately a very slight curvature across the

width can be beneficial, but don't overdo it as, while the joint looks good from the outside, there would be an appreciable gap down the centre of the joint with a consequent loss of strength.

A curvature of about 0.25mm at the centre of the blade would be acceptable. For general flattening work, the blade can be straight, with just the corners relieved slightly to avoid digging in. *See fig 1 for more graphic details of sharpening.*

In general, knives can be treated the same way as described, but much depends on type. In my particular trade, the majority of my assortment of knives have an equal bevel on either side, but as always the dreaded rounding over at the cutting edge, with its consequent loss of control, is to be avoided like the plague!

● After graduating from the Newark School of Violin Making in 1977, DOMINIC EXCELL set up his own workshop in Brighton. Since moving to Norfolk in 1988 he has continued to run the occasional, part-time and full-time courses which he began in Brighton.

LEFT: Bench oil-stone and slip stone (medium Arkansas pictured).

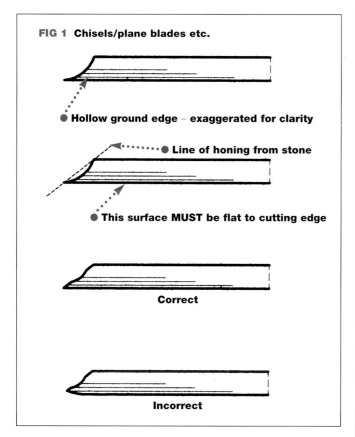

FIG 1 Chisels/plane blades etc.

● Hollow ground edge – exaggerated for clarity

● Line of honing from stone

● This surface MUST be flat to cutting edge

Correct

Incorrect

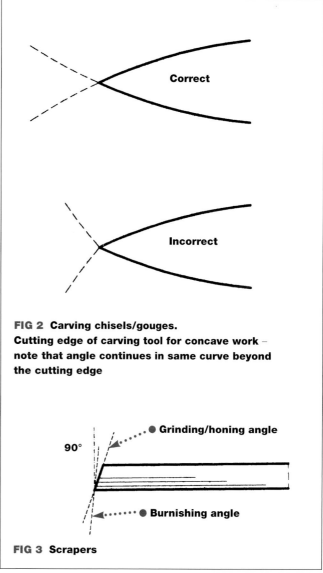

Correct

Incorrect

FIG 2 Carving chisels/gouges.
Cutting edge of carving tool for concave work –
note that angle continues in same curve beyond
the cutting edge

90°

● Grinding/honing angle

● Burnishing angle

FIG 3 Scrapers

"The dreaded rounding over at the cutting edge, with its consequent loss of control, is to be avoided like the plague"

Gouges

The same principles apply to sharpening gouges as for sharpening any other edge tool; that is a hollow-ground edge bridged over by the sharpening stone, but with a rounded slip-stone used to polish the 'flat' inner surface. It can be very useful to finish off with a leather strop.

A strop can be easily made by gluing a piece of leather to a scrap of wood which is curved to fit the gouge like a slip-stone, and coated with jewellers' rouge. Don't use too much pressure when polishing the edge, as the leather tends to compress under it only to expand as the tool passes, thus resulting in the aforementioned rounded over edge which is so difficult to work with.

Occasionally, a rounded edge is required on a chisel or gouge for some aspects of wood carving, especially where a marked concavity is required. In this instance, by all means allow the sides to be rounded, but avoid rounding the cutting edge still further, *as in fig 2*.

Cabinet scraper

The principles of sharpening cabinet scrapers are, contrary to popular opinion, no different from the sharpening of any other edge tool – a chisel for example – at least for the primary stage. The flat, polished underside should have its cutting edge ground back to about 75° to 80°, compared with the 25° to 30° for the chisel. Sharpen as for the chisel, using a medium/fine oil stone, ending the primary sharpening with a blunt-angled chisel edge.

This edge must now be burred over with a burnishing tool. This is simply a piece of hard, polished steel – the back of a well-polished gouge is very effective – which is firmly but with not too much pressure run around this cutting edge, at an angle approximately half way between the ground angle and right angles.

Assuming a grinding angle of 80°, the angle required for the burnisher would be $90° – \{(90 - 80)/2\}° = 85°$. *See fig 3.*

This secondary sharpening with the burnisher does not work too well the first time, but if repeated after first burnishing the flat underside – making certain that you do not round this edge over – it will usually give very good results. I imagine that the action of the burnisher against the scraper must slightly 'work harden' the cutting edge.

When the scraper starts to lose its edge, this secondary sharpening can be repeated seven or eight times before primary sharpening is required again.

I hope the methods outlined will be useful, but expect to practise to obtain the best results. ■

Ultimate acc

ACCURATE MEASUREMENT is fundamental to fine woodworking and, while steel expanding tape and conventional rules have their place, sometimes only absolute precision will do.

Enter the vernier callipers. These instruments come in three basic types – traditional engraved scale, dial or clock, and digital electronic – and cost anything from £10 for a plastic version up to £100 for a top-of-the-range electronic digital model.

They all consist of the same basic components, a fixed scale on the main bar of the calliper and a sliding scale that runs on it. Onto these two parts are attached the main jaws for external measuring, smaller pointed jaws for internal measuring and a depth gauge that emerges from the end of the main bar.

Regardless of cost, type, or user-friendliness, all these precision instruments must be treated with care and respect and must never be forced – they're not adjustable spanners!

Engraved scale

The engraved scale is the most common – the modern 'satin-finish' type being easier to read than the older 'bright-finish'. Their major drawback,

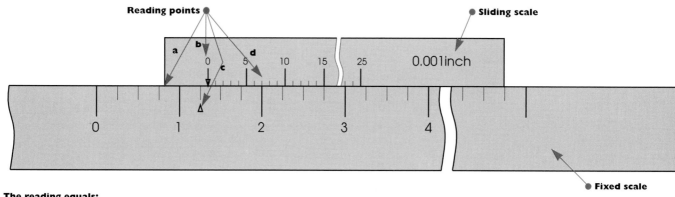

The reading equals:

Fixed scale					
	reading point a	nil x whole inches	=	0.000in	
	reading point b	1 x 0.100 inches	=	0.100in	
	reading point c	1 x 0.025 inches	=	0.025in	
Sliding scale to fixed scale @ unit 7					
	reading point d	7 x 0.001 inches	=	0.007in	
		Total	=	0.132inch	

ABOVE: Fig A Engraved scale vernier calliper
Resolution = 0.001in

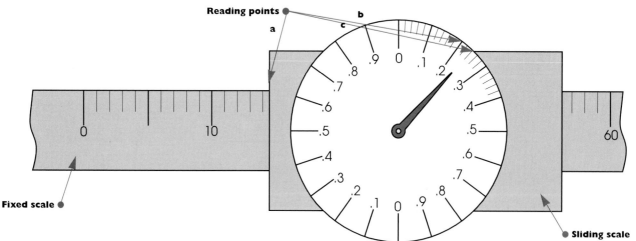

The reading equals:

Fixed scale				
	reading point a	14 x 1mm	=	14.00mm
	reading point b	2 x 0.1mm	=	0.20mm
	reading point c	2 x 0.02mm	=	0.04mm
		Total	=	14.24mm

ABOVE: Fig B Dial calliper Resolution = 0.02mm

uracy

Bill Cain looks at vernier callipers

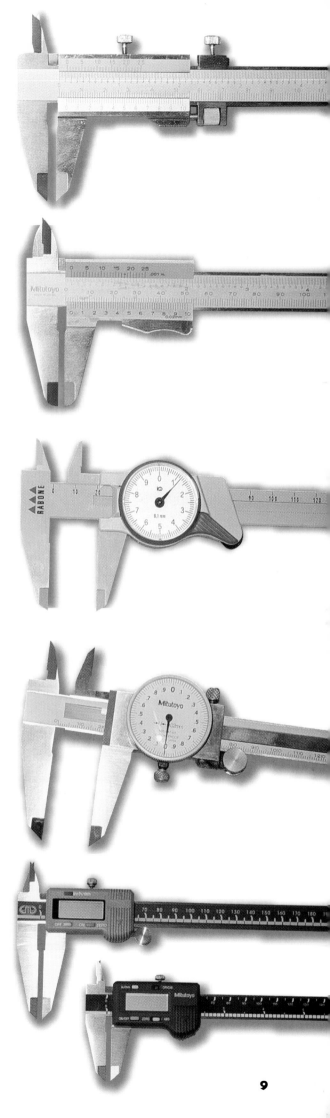

however, is a reliance on the lining-up of the engraved scale lines for reading, meaning that parallax errors can occur if the calliper is not viewed square on.

If the available light is poor, or your eyesight is not too good, they can be a bit of a pain – I can no longer read one without a magnifying glass! They are, therefore, not as quick or easy to use as the dial or digital versions.

The reading is taken from the alignment of the engraved lines on the fixed scale relative to the sliding scale. For example, using an imperial calibration with a resolution of 0.001in – each 1in of the fixed scale is divided into 10 units and each of these 10 units is further divided into four sub-units, providing 0.100 and 0.025in increments.

The sliding scale is divided into 25 units, which enables the 0.025in units on the fixed scale to be further divided into 0.001in units.

In use

To use, read off on the fixed scale, relative to the 'zero' on the sliding scale:

1) The whole inches
2) The number of 0.100in units
3) The number of 0.025in units
4) By sighting from the fixed scale to the sliding scale, look for the point where the line on both scales coincides; at the point of alignment, read off the division on the sliding scale to give the number of 0.001in units.

The sum of the above is the vernier measurement reading.

The same principles are employed

ABOVE: The numerous uses of a vernier calliper include checking the thickness of man-made boards – is it 6mm or 0.25in?

ABOVE: Measuring a mortice with the internal jaws

RIGHT: From the top – Axminster engraved vernier calliper, Mitutoyo engraved, Rabone dial, an imported model dial, Axminster digital and Mitutoyo digital

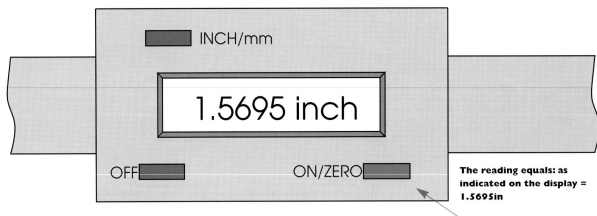

INCH/mm

1.5695 inch

OFF   ON/ZERO

The reading equals: as indicated on the display = 1.5695in

ABOVE: Fig C Digital or electronic calliper   Resolution = 0.0005

● **Sliding display and controls**

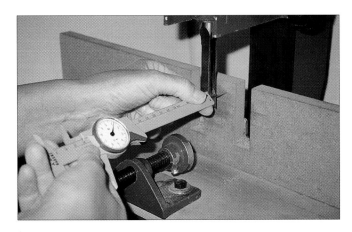

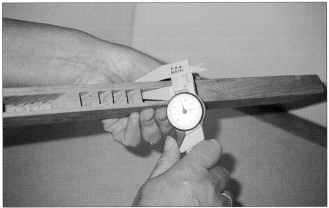

ABOVE: Setting a mortice chisel with the depth gauge

ABOVE RIGHT: Checking the position of a mortice offset with the main jaws

RIGHT: Measuring a tenon's haunch with the depth gauge

on a metrically scaled instrument, but the centimetre fixed scale is sub-divided into 10 units representing 1.0mm per division.

The sliding scale is graduated into 10 prime divisions, each representing 0.10mm. These are further divided into five sub-divisions to give a final resolution of 0.02mm per division.

Readings are taken as for an imperial instrument:
1) Read off on the fixed scale relative to the 'zero' on the sliding scale
2) The whole centimetres
3) The whole millimetres
4) At the point where the lines on the fixed and sliding scales align, read off on the sliding scale, remembering that each division on the scale represents 0.02mm.

Again, the sum of the readings equates to the measurement taken.

Dial or clock
A great improvement on the conventional version, as far as readability goes, is offered by dial or clock callipers. This style can read in either imperial or metric – some dual version are available, but to me their dials seem a bit cluttered.

Reading them is a simpler matter than reading the traditional version. A metric model has a resolution of 0.02mm.

To use:
1) Bring the measuring faces together
2) 'Zero' the dial by rotating its bezel

3) Read by reference from the sliding scale face to the fixed scale the whole millimetres; and from the dial read the number of 0.1mm divisions and the 0.02mm sub-divisions.

Again, the sum of the readings equates to the measurement taken.

Digital or electronic
The digital or electronic type, the most modern of the three, is powered by a disposable battery that is the size of a watch's and with a life that can be measured in years.

Instant imperial or metric reading is

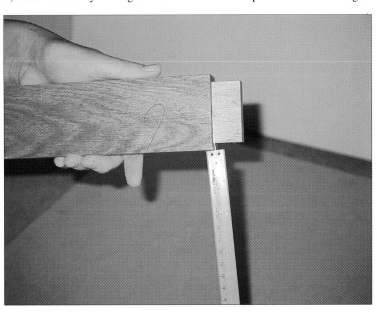

BUYING SECOND-HAND
Bargains can be turned up at tool stores or even car boot sales, but take care. To avoid picking up an inaccurate measuring instrument, check it out by comparing it with a known standard, such as the ground shank of a quality unused router cutter, or by comparison with other verniers.

Always check that slide and dial are free to move over their full ranges, and that measuring faces are damage-free and true by zeroing and holding the instrument up to the light.

Reject any digital instrument showing damage or display function problems.

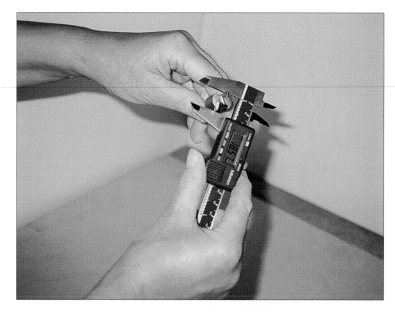

at the touch of a button so if, like me, you are not yet fully metricated, then this capability is great.

Despite owning other types, this is the instrument I use 99% of the time.

To use:

1) Bring the measuring faces together and press the 'zero' button; the display should now read either 0.00mm or 0.00in depending on the mode selected and the resolution of the instrument.

2) Take the required measurement; the display will show the achieved dimension.

The instrument can be zeroed at any point over its range so, for example, a shaft-to-hole fit can be instantly established without recourse to mathematics.

Accuracy test

When trying out the various types of vernier calliper, I adopted the Mitutoyo Digimatic as a comparison standard.

All my samples, *see panel*, were accurate to their stated resolution.

I suspect that the measuring faces of the plastic Rabone dial version would need to be treated with a little extra respect, but for use on wood I don't see this as a problem. You get what you pay for, and plastic versions must be regarded as budget instruments intended for light use.

For the reasons already stated I would place in order of preference:

1) Digital
2) Dial
3) Conventional

You must choose make, model, and supplier based on intended use, resolution required, and budget. All I advise is that you go for a model offering a slide lock plus, if possible, fine adjustment – and make it the best that you can afford.■

LEFT: Accurately measuring the diameter of a router cutter

LEFT: Checking the thickness of a freshly planed piece of wood

BELOW: The digital calliper relies on batteries which will need changing – but not too often

MAKES AND MODELS

Traditional engraved scale

Axminster	WEZ6197F, thumblock, 0.02mm (0.001in) model	£28.90*
Mitutoyo	133001, thumblock, 0.02mm (0.001in) model	£39.24*

Dial

Stanley Rabone	RAB699, plastic, 0.1mm (0.004in) model	£15.61*
Imported model	388004, 0.02mm (0.01in) model	£30.50

Digital electric

Axminster	388006, 0.01mm (0.0005in) model	£49.35
Mitutoyo	MIT500133U, 0.01mm (0.0005in) model	£99.95*

* denotes pricing for 150mm (6in) callipers
All prices include VAT

Thanks to Axminster Power Tool Centre who loaned us the samples used in this article.
Contact: Axminster Power Tool Centre, Chard Street, Axminster, Devon EX13 5DZ
Tel: 01297 33656 Fax: 01297 35242

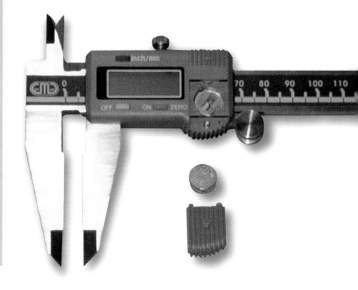

ABOVE: Tambour
doors in this
buffet combine
elegance with
ease of access.
Photograph by
Phillip Nilsson

On a roll

Richard Wedler provides a simple solution to fitting
doors where space is limited

PHOTOGRAPHY BY
SANDOR NAGYSZALNCZY

THE FIRST TIME I chose to incorporate tambour doors in a furniture project I turned to an 'old-timer' who helped me to establish a few practical guidelines.

My client had asked me to build a dining buffet to complement an existing table, but it had to be fitted into a confined space. The commission required a long, shallow piece with radiused ends.

As my friend pointed out, the restricted floor space between table and buffet would make hinged doors awkward; sliding doors would further reduce the already minimal storage depth.

So horizontal tambours seemed not only the most natural choice, but would make an attractive design feature too.

I found that the canvas-backed tambour process provides a simple solution to door management, but that, like any other cabinet or furniture project, success is as dependent on planning as on execution.

In the 15 years since, I have realised the importance of considering the capability of the piece to accommodate the tambour pathway.

The most accessible tambour projects involve gentle curves and allow door removal from the rear, so that the canvas/slat assemblies can be slid into their tracks.

Cabinet plans with radiused

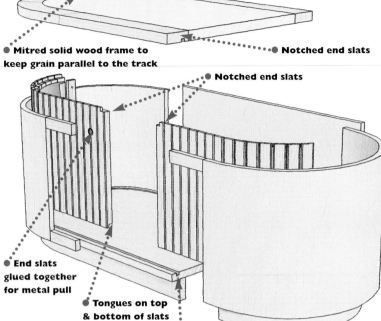

- ● **Mitred solid wood frame to keep grain parallel to the track**
- ● **Notched end slats**
- ● **Notched end slats**
- ● **End slats glued together for metal pull**
- ● **Tongues on top & bottom of slats ride in grooves**
- ● **Bottom track**

"The old theory involving the path of least resistance is paramount"

ends or fronts lend themselves to horizontal tambour doors, but rectilinear carcasses can also be fitted if the slot in which the doors travel provides a smooth movement. I have seen tambours that follow radii as small as 25mm, 1in with ease.

Scale layout

A full-scale layout in plan view drawn on a heavy paper allows the subsequent generation of templates and the derivation of sizes for individual parts of the piece.

Elevation and section plans can be done in scale, and, with rough dimensions determined, the slats can be milled, *see panel*.

A design consideration worth mentioning is the sequential cutting of the tambours to preserve grain patterns in the finished door. Although this represents a great deal more work — and librarian-like organisation — the results are extremely rewarding.

The carcass

With the milled slats set aside, attention is turned to a pathway in the carcass that will permit the doors to move smoothly.

Finer pieces are traditionally accomplished by creating a solid wood surround to allow a slot to be cut with as little end grain as possible, but on our radius we decided on a hexagon format, *see drawing*, gluing up a frame of the same material as the tambours into which the radius was cut and mated to the cabinet's floor.

At this point care must be taken to avoid exposing the dowel or spline when the tambour slot is generated.

Although it is desirable to use this construction for both the top and bottom of the carcass, the bottom is the more important, since most resistance occurs here during door travel.

'Inner cabinet'

An 'inner cabinet' will be required for the support of any shelving and to prevent objects placed in the cabinet from interfering with the movement of the tambours. This means that the tambour track must be planned to provide adequate clearances from both inner and outer carcasses.

When planning the best path for the routed pathway on the full-scale layout, remember that the more graceful the curve, the smoother the doors will operate; so consider not only the path of travel, but also the point of installation and/or removal.

A removable back can easily be accomplished by allowing the slot to fade gently out of the back of the cabinet. Once the tambour slats are glued up on their canvas backing they will bend significantly in only one direction.

My 'old-timer' friend taught me one additional refinement: to let the slot drift toward the front of the door opening so as to minimise the tambour set-back when closed.

This is accomplished by tapering the face frame that surrounds the door opening; the result is a fine, more sophisticated appearance to the piece, particularly with horizontal doors.

Slot template

With the planning done, cutting the tambour slot is relatively simple. 6mm, 1/4in MDF is

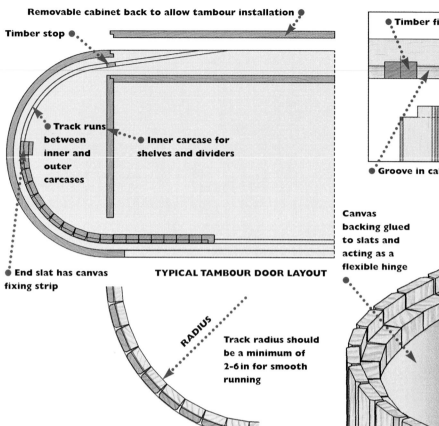

Removable cabinet back to allow tambour installation ●

Timber stop ●

● Track runs between inner and outer carcases

● Inner carcase for shelves and dividers

● End slat has canvas fixing strip

TYPICAL TAMBOUR DOOR LAYOUT

RADIUS

Track radius should be a minimum of 2-6 in for smooth running

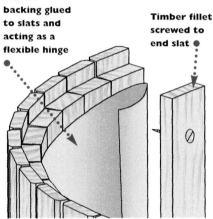

● Timber fillet screwed to end slat

● Groove in cabinet top

Canvas backing glued to slats and acting as a flexible hinge

Timber fillet screwed to end slat ●

● At various times an award-winning film maker and guitarist, but always a professional woodworker, RICHARD WEDLER lives and works in Los Angeles. The son of an inventor, he spent childhood weekends cabinetmaking and went on to make furniture for Hollywood notables including Bob Hope. He is currently spending most of his time marketing his Micro Fence, *see Toolbox this issue,* but looks forward to dividing his time more evenly between that and furniture-making.

perfectly adequate for a template.

This can be cut with the help of the full-scale layout, allowing for the width of the wall of the template guide-bushing.

First, select the size and type of cutter to be used for the cut — I've had particularly good luck with TCT slotting cutters, though standard TCT two flute cutters will prove adequate.

For most doors 6mm, $^1/_4$in or 8mm, $^5/_{16}$in is a convenient size to work with, though sizes up to 10mm, $^3/_8$in might be appropriate for larger doors.

Remember that the final result is an end-grain tongue sliding along a flat-grain track, and that the old theory involving the path of least resistance is paramount.

With the cutter and guide bush set up in the router, make a test cut to check the dimension of the set-back to be incorporated in the template.

When the router template is cut and smoothly sanded, mark its top permanently, being careful not to flip it when cutting the top and bottom of the carcass. Mark positional references for the template on top, bottom and opposing ends of the cabinet; a simple centre-line on both template and carcasses may be all that is necessary.

The pathway slots can be cut

and thoroughly sanded once the template is clamped or tacked securely to the appropriate carcass member.

Some makers suggest that pre-assembly lubrication of the slot may be advisable — particularly when interior cabinet structure may prevent access after assembly — but care should be taken over the finish of the piece.

Assembly jig
With the cabinet assembled, the pathway slot routed and sanded, and the tambour slats 'settled in' to straightness, the door assembly can be prepared.

Make up an assembly board, trapping the slats on three sides, with the fourth clamping the grouping of slats firmly together.

Each of the sides surrounding the tambours should be of lesser thickness, allowing the slats to protrude 1.5mm, $^1/_{16}$in or so above, and permit the spread of glue to cover only the tambours, not the jig. If the canvas is to be clamped after bonding, *see panel,* the lower jig will not interfere.

Gluing tambours
Tambours are now selected from the stickers for perfect straightness, and cut to equal length before being clamped tightly face down in the

assembly jig.

I like to draw pencil lines on the tambour backs and canvas material to guide the glue spread — usually held back 19mm, $^3/_4$in or so from the slat ends. An extra 100 or 125mm, 4 or 5in at each end of the canvas is left adhesive-free, to allow the canvas to be held down flat via batten boards while the glue is applied, and to provide flaps which can later be doubled back and secured with a backing piece of wood to prevent the material unravelling.

With the glue spread and dry

> "When fluid motion in the slots is achieved, a fine sanding should give you 'pinkie-finger' operation"

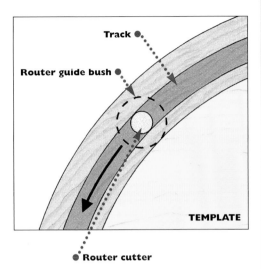

Track

Router guide bush

TEMPLATE

Router cutter

MACHINING TAMBOUR SLATS

THIS PROCESS REQUIRES particular patience and accuracy — generosity might be an operative word here too. Experience has taught me to add at least 25 to 30% to the slat count, depending on the type of timber used and the accuracy achieved in machining narrow strips.

I like to start by machining stock at least 1½ times the thickness and width of the finished slat, and conduct a gradual milling process that occurs in a number of stages.

ABOVE: During the machining process up to 30% of slats will be discarded

With rough-cut stock, the first stage involves planing and thicknessing to roughly 130 to 140% of finished size. With ready-planed material, a simple straightening and thicknessing will suffice.

Either way, the next step is to place these slat candidates in stick, allowing air flow on all sides while they become accustomed to their new, smaller dimension. Some might warp, bend or twist slightly, but enough stock is left on each piece to allow for corrections in the next milling step.

Drying time depends on stabilisation. This varies according to species and climate, but most adjustment will probably have happened within a few days.

The next step is to take the stock down another 15% or so by re-planing two adjacent edges and re-thicknessing or table-sawing the remaining two.

After this step, it's back to the sticks for another wait.

The last machining stage takes the slats to within a sanding of the final dimensions, this time employing finer settings. To remove any remaining warp and to leave the cleanest tear-free cut possible, the planer should be adjusted to a scant 0.8mm, ¹/₃₂in.

If considerable material removal is indicated by the chosen slat shape, accomplish this prior to any final sizings, so avoiding additional warping or twisting.

Our workshop is blessed with a small, though pampered, drum sander that provides the final preparation of our tambours, though even a block-and-paper approach could give the desired results.

After this final sanding, set the slats aside on their sticks to await the making of the doors. Edge detailing should be accomplished prior to door assembly, along with a final fine sanding.

---

assembly can begin. With the help of pencil outlines and another pair of hands, the canvas can be smoothed down on the slats and any wrinkles or bumps worked out with the aid of a laminate roller or a veneer hammer.

Firm, even pressure will probably result in an adequate bond, but if in doubt, or if yellow glue – aliphatic resin – has been used, clamp a flat board on top for a few hours, with a membrane of cling film or paper to prevent any bonding to the back of the canvas.

After removing the assembly from the jig, check each joint to ensure that it bends freely.

Fitting doors

With door assembly complete, the tongues can be rebated top and bottom, with care taken to dimension them for the smoothest movement possible in their grooves.

The rabbet is usually let into the front of the door — opposite the canvas — to conceal the slot. With a moulded detail or half-round variety of tambour, the front rabbet helps hide the groove in the adjoining recesses, and eliminates the possibility of wear showing up in the finish at the top and bottom of the tambours.

Assuming the front rabbet is used, I prefer to use a table saw with a sharp dado head set to the shy side of estimated dimensions.

By trial and error at the carcass, the best working dimensions can be accomplished through subsequent 'shim' cuts.

Overall tongue-to-tongue dimension should include adequate clearance to prevent binding — maybe 1.5mm, ¹/₁₆in or so — and the rebated shoulders should also give a pleasing reveal; somewhere around 1.5 to 3mm,¹/₁₆ to ¹/₈in.

When fluid motion in the slots is achieved, a fine sanding should give you 'pinkie-finger' operation; easing the edges of the tongues may help.

Handle design

The canvas ends can now be secured and trimmed on the back of the doors, and the handle

design addressed. Some tambours can be capped with a larger end piece, with a finger pull cut in or a handle attached.

Alternatively, two or three slats at the leading edge of the door can be glued together to provide a solid backing into which a ring pull might be routed.

Finally, having maximised the smoothness of motion, stops at the rear of the doors' slot may be fitted. In the case of double-door cabinets, stops ensure a proper stopping location in the closed position.

This job can be accomplished at the top invisibly by notching the tongue of the first tambour slat and installing a stop block.

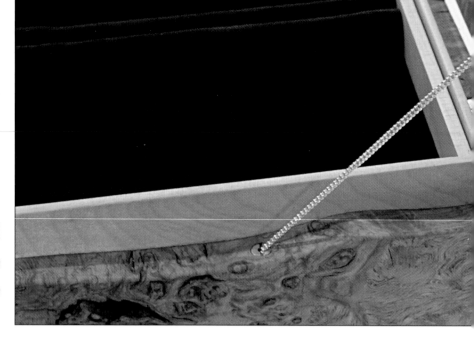

Box maker **Peter Lloyd** extols the delights of the wooden hinge

Pivotal movem

● **Former craft design technology teacher PETER LLOYD** turned to making boxes at his home in Brampton, Cumbria after returning from teaching in Botswana some eight years ago. He specialises in jewellery boxes, work boxes and writing slopes constructed from woods like ripple ash, ripple sycamore and burr elm.

I HAD WANDERED, by who knows what quirk of fate, into In Design in Chester and was instantly smitten. Even now, many years on, I can still remember being awe-struck by the warren of rooms displaying, for the most part, the amazing furniture of Tim Stead, *see F&C No. 6.*

That was my first sight of a wooden hinge, and I'm quite sure that somewhere deep within me some sort of seed was planted.

My first box didn't actually have wooden hinges at all. Conventional silver-plated brass butts did the business. The beautiful piece of burr elm that I was using was far from conventional, however, and

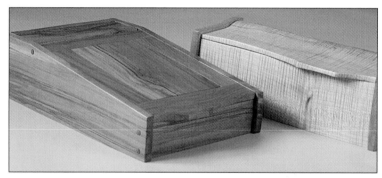

ABOVE: **Photo 4 The hinge featured on this computer disc box and writing slope features wooden pivots and 'stops' provided by the shape of the lids**

although I didn't realise it at the time it was begging for an altogether more rugged hinge, *see photo 1.*

Chest hinge
A Waywood chest was to indicate the path ahead, *see panel.*

My first wooden hinge was basically a chest hinge in wood,

LEFT AND BELOW: **Photos 2 & 3 Waywood-inspired wooden chest hinges**

see photos 2 and 3. A router was used with a Leigh jig to cut the slots; holes were drilled from both sides and the ends were radiused. These hinges had to be square and perfectly aligned in all planes in order to function, and more often than not they weren't. This necessitated many tedious hours of taking them off, shaving the high spots, refitting and repeating the whole process until they worked.

Nowadays I drill the hole first; if it runs off line – which it usually does – the machine vice can be tilted slightly and the hole redrilled, *see fig 1.*

The slots are cut with a router mounted in an inversion table, the hinge being clamped to a mitre fence and passed across the cutter. Radiusing is then accomplished by means of a jig

LEFT: Waywood box

"To my mind a wooden hinge has got to be something more than just a large version of a metal one"

ent

on the sanding disc, *see fig 2*.

The hinges are next counter bored and screwed to the lid and back for checking; if everything operates smoothly the knuckles are sanded and the pivot pin glued in place.

Simpler affair

Mark II hinge is an altogether simpler affair, *see photo 4 of computer disk box and writing slope*. It comprises a wooden pivot in the end of the lid, the 'stop' being provided by the shape of the lid, *see fig 3*.

The sides are drilled before the box is glued up; the lid is planed and sanded to an exact fit and then drilled, ensuring that the drill is parallel to the top and back. The pegs are planed from square section material with a slight taper.

The lid can then be checked for satisfactory operation before the pegs are pushed home with a drop of glue and cut to length. This approach was detailed in F&C No. 1.

Cut into two

Another of my hinges – used on the back of a box – is cut in the same way as the first; but both halves of this one are radiused, *see photo 5*. The box is made in the traditional way, with the lid and bottom fixed. The back is then routed out to the exact width

BARNABY SCOTT of Waywood recalls: "We first started to make wooden hinges when we were doing a series of sculptured chests. They were each shaped differently, but all had a distinctly organic feel that was heightened by the choice of wood and finish – generally elm or oak – and the oil and/or wax finishes that we use exclusively.

"The organic, woody character of these pieces seemed to cry out against the use of standard metal – especially brass – hardware which we woodworkers so often reach for without thinking.

"Thus the Waywood version of the wooden hinge was born. We were well aware that wooden hinges had been made for centuries, but deliberately did no research into them so that we could design and make our own versions uninhibitedly."

ABOVE: This Waywood hinge is an integral part of the design of this curvaceous box

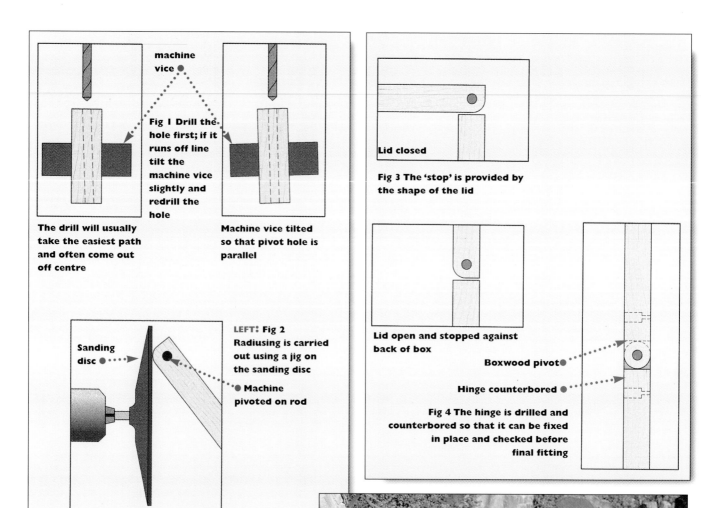

Fig 1 Drill the hole first; if it runs off line tilt the machine vice slightly and redrill the hole

machine vice

The drill will usually take the easiest path and often come out off centre

Machine vice tilted so that pivot hole is parallel

Sanding disc

LEFT: Fig 2 Radiusing is carried out using a jig on the sanding disc

Machine pivoted on rod

Lid closed

Fig 3 The 'stop' is provided by the shape of the lid

Lid open and stopped against back of box

Boxwood pivot

Hinge counterbored

Fig 4 The hinge is drilled and counterbored so that it can be fixed in place and checked before final fitting

"Because I love the idea of the all wood box I am always looking for new ways of making hinges"

ABOVE RIGHT:
Photo 7 Bold hinges on this Tim Stead cabinet

of the hinge so that the box can be cut into two.

The hinge is drilled and counterbored so that it can be fixed in place and checked before being finally fitted, *see fig 4*.

Jig device

Recently I looked at a hinge-making device which is fairly new on the market, but to describe it as a jig is perhaps a bit of an overstatement; all you get for your money is a set of instructions and a block of aluminium to guide a drill bit.

My quarrel with this device is that it produces only a wooden butt hinge – wood copying metal! To my mind a wooden hinge has got to be something more than just a large version of a metal one.

Because I love the idea of the all wood box I am always looking for new ways of making hinges. Every time I find one I'm foolish enough to think that there can't possibly be any more ways of pivoting a wooden lid – but then along comes another.

WOODEN HINGE SPONSOR

TIM STEAD tells me that Alan Brown, the extraordinary force behind In Design, promoted the wooden hinge: "While he was always positive and excited about a piece he always wanted to question it, to push it forward and improve it."

Sadly Alan Brown has died, but it is clear that his enthusiasm and spirit still shine clear and bright.

ABOVE: Photo 6 An example of Alan Brown's work

Extension table

Richard Jones makes a draw leaf run-off table for his Wadkin CP15 table saw

● **RICHARD JONES** trained as a cabinetmaker and, after some years as a craftsman with furniture workshops, spent nine years teaching MA students of Furniture Design & Craft at Heriot Watt University in Edinburgh. He specialises in the design and production of fine contemporary pieces as well as antique restoration, and is now settled in the USA

ABOVE RIGHT: Cross-cutting with extensions down allows full use of carriage

I OWN A WADKIN CPI5 table saw with a factory fitted sliding table for handling panels and other cros-cutting operations. The panel-handling capacity, and facility to cut such things as dihedral angles, is enormous – along with ripping capabilities, and the added benefit that the sliding table splits at the sawblade. This reduces the chance of a board being tipped into the back of the sawblade due to friction, producing ruined cuts and kickbacks.

Outfeed support
Nearly every furniture workshop has devised some means to extend the outfeed support for cut material as it passes by the blade and off the end of the saw. In many cutting operations an unsupported cut piece will

> "Nearly every furniture workshop has devised some means to extend the outfeed support for cut material as it passes by the blade and off the end of the saw"

dangerously cantilever off the typical factory saw bench, unless you have an auxiliary table to prevent this.

My machine, like most of its type, has something of an Achilles heel – which is the question of what to use for a run-off table. The problem is twofold – how to make an auxiliary table that, during rip-ping operations, is suitable for catching both what is being dimensioned to the right of the

sawblade as well as the off-cut which is to the left, and how to support off-cuts produced during panel sizing operations when they are to the right of the blade!

Problem
Dragging an auxiliary run-off table across the floor is inconvenient and it will generally be the wrong height. Free standing rollers have similar problems to unattached run-offs,

LEFT: Ripping made safer with table at its full capacity

especially when a plank is warped and drops down off the end of the saw table into the gaps between the rollers.

I have messed about with drop-leaf and fold-up tables where part of the table is permanently set to the right of the saw blade, but found that dust, waste, and off-cuts become trapped between the leaves.

"A major advantage of this type of run-off table is that all the dust and scraps are swept off the draw leaves by the main table top as the leaves are pushed home, so that damage to hinges and other parts is eliminated"

LEFT: Set-up for ripping wider stock with one leaf extended

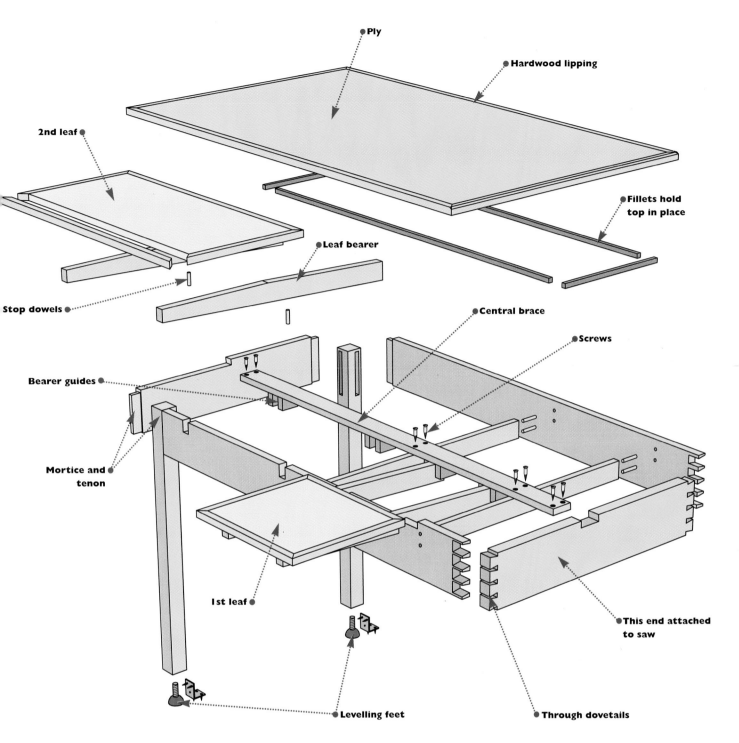

- • Ply
- • Hardwood lipping
- • 2nd leaf
- • Fillets hold top in place
- • Stop dowels
- • Leaf bearer
- • Central brace
- • Screws
- • Bearer guides
- • Mortice and tenon
- • 1st leaf
- • This end attached to saw
- • Levelling feet
- • Through dovetails

Solution

I designed a simple two legged draw leaf table that attaches to the outfeed end of my Wadkin cast iron table which permanently provides support for material as it passes by the right side of the sawblade. Two leaves pull out, when needed, from underneath the main top to support the offcut on the left side of the sawblade. Having two draw leaves is specific to this machine because I can set the sliding table in two positions for ripping operations.

A major advantage of this type of run-off table is that all the dust and scraps are swept off the draw leaves by the main table top as the leaves are pushed home, so that damage to hinges and other parts is eliminated.

Naturally, there is still one minor disadvantage, but it is one I am happy to live with – I must walk around the machine to extend or close the leaves depending on the mode of operation!

Design

In designing my run-off table I took into account how I use my machine and for what purposes. The following points will help you to adapt the basic concept for your specific requirements.

Adjust the leg length to suit the saw height and floor level.

I have two draw leaves but one may be all you need, particularly if the sliding table can only

handle boards up to 1220mm (48in) wide.

The length of run-off table should be adjusted to suit the longest length of material you normally cut.

I have found that the 350mm (13¾in) wide draw leaves are more than adequate to support solid wood off-cuts during ripping. As a general rule make the overall width no more than about 800mm (31⅛in). This will just support a 3000 x 1500mm (10 x 5ft) piece of MDF cut in half across the width.

If you use heavy boards you may need to increase the width of the rails which would allow an increase in the width of the leaf bearers to take the strain.

It would be necessary to attach the rails to the legs with forked extended mortices and shorter width tenons, gluing only the upper part of the forked tenons so as to prevent splitting of the rail due to seasonal wood movement – confining this movement to the lower part of the rail. This maintains the level correctly at the top, where it matters for the table top and leaves. The height of the bottom edge of the rail can move up and down causing no change in the top height in relationship to the saw table height.

Additional intermediate cross rails should be added according to what you assess the abuse to your run-off table will be. They stiffen the central long running leaf bearer, so preventing the draw leaves from drooping by supporting the centre of the main top, and breakage to the leaf bearer itself. The intermediate bearers can be any width up to the width of the outside rails.

I found that the humidity here in Houston did nasty things to the large top; it warped it so that the leading edge sat proud of the edge of the saw table itself. I cured this problem by adding two bits of screwed-on plywood to the rail bolted to the saw table, hooks, and springs, to hold the leading edge of the top down. You may not need this – I suggest you wait and see before adding it.The construction requires some elementary variations on the draw leaf table theme. The essential variation being that half a drawer leaf table is to be constructed, therefore the rails on the non leaf side of the structure must be increased in width by the thickness of the leaf that pulls out, that is, by 18 mm (¾in).

> "Naturally, there is still one minor disadvantage, but it is one I am happy to live with – I must walk around the machine to extend or close the leaves depending on the mode of operation"

Construction

The choice of materials is down to what you have around. Quality ply and a tough hardwood are good.

Once the materials are cut to size, lay out a full size rod so that the correct angles and profiles are precisely plotted. This helps with the cut outs and their angles on the long rail and trimming the leaf bearers to fit the leaves.

Cut the notched width reduction in the short rail to match the thickness of your board material. Cut the notch in the other short rail to suit the central bearer.

Mortice and tenon the two long rails and one short rail to the legs – doweling or biscuits might suffice. Lay out and cut through the dovetails at the rail ends.

Next, bore holes in the bottom of the legs to accept the T nuts and levellers. Then make the central leaf bearer and dry fit all the parts you have so far produced, and temporarily screw them together.

Four notches now need to be formed in the long rail to accept the leaf bearers. The notches should be cut a shade wider than the bearers and angled down towards the floor on the inside of the rail framework. The exact angle must be gained from your rod. Now mark and cut them.

Glue together the rails, legs, and dovetailed rail ends, and glue and screw the central leaf bearer.

ABOVE:
**Underneath with
leaves extended –
note springs for
holding down tops
inclined to warp**

BELOW:
Bearer guides

Intermediate cross rails are attached to the long rails and to the underside of the central leaf bearer, their purpose being to stiffen the structure. Cut them to the exact internal dimension between the long rails. Screw and glue them permanently to the underside of the central leaf bearer and temporarily through, from the outside of the long rails, into their long grain.

When the glue has gone off, remove the temporary screws from the long rails, bore into the existing screw holes and glue in 9 mm (⅜in) dowels, flushing them off afterwards.

Top

Make the top and leaves next and attach the lipping, using biscuits or tongues.

Using the rod, precisely shape the leaf bearers to fit to the underside of the draw leaves, central leaf bearer, and long notched rail.

Attach the main table top to the rail and leg structure. Fix the fillets permanently to the underside of the top with glue and screws, allowing for a bit of movement.

Slip the draw leaves in place. Set the leaf bearers on the leaves so that they extend through the notches in the rail.

They should now be just shy of the back rail. Mark their position ensuring that they are parallel, and slip the leaves back out. Bore and counterbore screw holes as needed so that the screws don't come through the leaf top, and dry assemble these parts.

Put the leaves and their bearers back in place and attach the leaf bearer guides to the underside of the central leaf bearer with glue and screws.

Support the legless end, and test the movement of the leaves. While the leaves are fully extended, mark where the inside of the front rail coincides with the leaf bearers. This is where the leaf stop dowels are fitted. Bore and glue these in place. Allow only a smidgen of sloppiness.

Attaching

The table has to be attached to the saw, and how you do this will depend upon your saw's make and model. If there are pre–tapped holes already in place on the edge of the saws table, use them. If not, drill and tap holes to suit. I recommend that you use two slotted holes in the short rail for fine tuning the height, and two round holes to permanently fix the table once this height has been established. There may well be some packing and shimming to do for cast iron tops are rarely absolutely square and flat.

Adjust the height of the far end of the outfeed table exactly to the saw table height with the T nuts and levellers and fix permanently to the floor with angle brackets, screws and rawlplugs.

Plane a low angled chamfer or gently round over the leading edge of the main top and the draw leaf. If they move a little due to dust build up or warpage, off-cuts won't bang dangerously into a hard corner, and are guided up onto the run-off table.

Finish

Polish or varnish the tops and bearers. This helps reduce damage and seasonal movement, and allows rough timber to slide over the leaves more easily. Candle wax can be rubbed on moving parts to reduce friction. ∎

Ripping yarns

Paul Richardson and **Alan Goodsell** on the virtues and vices of the most versatile machine in the workshop

PHOTOGRAPHY BY
ANTHONY BAILEY

SPACE MACHINE

THERE IS A bewildering variety of machines available to the furniture-maker these days, and no-one will have a full set of all of them. In fact no-one should have a full set; Anthony Bailey and I once worked for a firm whose workshop had been equipped with more enthusiasm than thoughtfulness; the machine shop was packed with gleaming machinery that couldn't be used because there wasn't room for a piece of wood!

The first chance we had – ironically while the proprietor was recovering from a sawbench injury – half the equipment was put into storage. This simple move doubled efficiency and safety.

Versatility
The main object of our reshuffle was to create working space around the big Startrite panel saw. The table saw is at the heart of any machine shop – every workpiece used, whether solid timber or sheet material, goes through it at least once – and will, therefore, be in use for more of the time than any other single piece of equipment.

Consider the versatility of the tool: it is initially used to rip raw timber to cutting-list components,

> "Give this most versatile of machines room to breathe and it will process more work for you than all your other equipment put together"

Dangerous ripping practice illustrated* – Guard and riving knife missing, blade too low, fence extended too far, clutter on table, no push stick, long hair and loose clothing – the operator is also standing in line with the cut, see main text

The correct approach to ripping

*Please note: our 'dangerous practice' pictures were p•

then once planed they are back for cross-cutting to length; it will dimension sheet materials like MDF; it will mitre, bevel, groove, rebate, tenon, finger-joint, house and otherwise joint components.

Beyond these basic uses lie hundreds of specialist operations which can be carried out on the table saw with ingenuity and a few jigs to suit the needs of the individual. In this way knuckle-joints can be made, for example, and even large cove mouldings can be formed by passing the work incrementally through a jig fixed diagonally across the saw.

Planning
So when planning a workshop, build it around a good table saw, preferably fitted with a good sliding carriage for accurate dimensioning and cross-cutting. Make sure that there is enough clear space around it to use its full potential; to process 2400mm, 8ft long boards the saw must have around 3000mm, 10ft in front of, behind and to the left of the blade. To rip up to 1200mm, 4ft in width it must also have 1400mm, 56in clear to the right of the blade; so ideally a table saw needs to sit in a space measuring 6000mm by 3800mm, 20ft by 12ft 6in.

This may well be impractical, but careful planning should allow other equipment to be sited in such a way that it can be moved when large boards are being sawn, or can be lower than the saw's table, allowing material to pass over it.

Whatever the constraints on space, give this most versatile of machines room to breathe and it will process more work for you than all your other equipment put together.

Paul Richardson

ABOVE: Thorough
guarding on a
machine from the
golden age

"Following a few simple guidelines will increase the chances of keeping all 10 digits"

Dangerous cross-cutting practice illustrated* – All the faults listed for ripping, plus indexing from the rip fence – trapping the offcut between fence and blade

The correct approach to cross-cutting, indexing from a stop on the cross-cut fence

h the machine static and isolated.

SAFETY FIRST

THE FIRST stage in any woodworking project is to convert natural tree-shaped boards into four-sided pieces of material, conveniently sized for each component. The sawbench or table saw is the correct machine for the job; its design is fundamental and normally includes only one exposed moving part – the blade.

Although simple, I have seen more fingers removed on these than on any other machine in the workshop. This may be due to its simplicity, inviting a lack of care and a disregard for safety that invites the machine to bite back – which it can do with alarming ferocity.

With this in mind great care must be taken when using a table saw as they can be unforgiving; following a few simple guidelines will increase the chances of keeping all 10 digits.

Dos & don'ts

Do ensure the sawblade is sharp, the resulting cut will be more accurate and reduce further finishing. A blunt blade will make pushing wood through the saw difficult, increasing the chance of a mishap.

Don't rush – take the time to set up properly.

Do make sure all guards are in position and the dust extractor is running before the saw is switched on.

Don't leave clutter on the bed of the saw, this includes offcuts, spanners, tape measures and cups of tea. Vibration will inevitably rattle one of these into the sawblade or cause a loss of concentration with dire results.

Do wear the correct safety gear; scratch-free goggles, ear defenders and a dust mask.

Don't wear loose clothing or jewellery – and if a stranger to the barber, tie long hair back and

tuck it out of the way.

Do set the blade as far above the bed as possible, so the cutting action is in a downward direction against the bed – a blade set too low will tend to force the timber back towards the operator. If possible stand slightly to one side of the cutting line so that if the worst happens and the timber does come shooting back, it won't ruin your chances of fatherhood.

Don't pull wood through a saw from behind the blade, particularly if you are taking-off for an operator, as there is a possibility that you will pull his hands onto a moving blade – which he will not thank you for.

Do use a push-stick when running wood through a saw, it is an obvious extension to your hands that won't drip blood if it accidentally touches the blade. Either use a proprietary example or, if making your own, ensure the notch is sufficient to hook over the end of the wood with a firm hold.

Don't pull out those loose slivers of wood that sometimes lodge themselves beside the blade until the machine has stopped running and is isolated from the mains supply.

Ripping tip

The fence position is often seen incorrectly positioned for ripping, *see picture.* It should extend no further than 25mm, 1in or so beyond the back of the blade to stop timber pinching between the blade and fence once it has been cut, again being thrown up and towards the operator.

Cross-cutting tip

Never, ever cross-cut so that the offcut is trapped between the blade and rip-fence, *see picture.* Always dimension timber from the free side of the blade using a stop on the cross-cut fence, and clear offcuts with a push stick immediately.

Safety & quality

Follow these simple tips and not only will the chance of finger survival be increased, but accuracy and quality of cut will be improved.

Alan Goodsell ■

Sawbench reborn

Putting his readers before personal pain, **Paul Richardson** forces himself to turn down the toes of a dead Startrite

T HERE IT SAT – laughing at me and rusting as I watched. The deceased Startrite TA175, which I had bought in a fit of misguided optimism, had been delivered. It was a depressing sight.

I toyed with the idea of throwing a sheet over it and forgetting it existed, but I had already told every reader of F&C that I would report on its progress. There was no escape; I was going to have to go through with it.

Starting point
The first thing to do with an old machine is much the same as should be done when starting any restoration – resist the urge to start taking it apart, and instead make a careful assessment of its condition and list the work that needs to be done.

> ## "Don't try moving anything that seems reluctant, as it is easy to shear a seized part"

Don't try moving anything that seems reluctant, as it is easy to shear a seized part – this had already happened to a stud on one of the bed bar extensions. After a visual check looking for obvious damage and missing components, saturate every nut, bolt and moving part with oil – not general purpose stuff, but a genuine penetrating oil such as Plus Gas. Leave to marinate for 24 hours.

Rust never sleeps
I was feeling more positive by this point. Visible damage was limited to the sheared stud and only one or two minor parts were missing. As expected, one of the rise-and-fall's universal joints had failed, *see photo*, but I intended to uprate both anyway.

The chief problem was rust. The cast-iron table looked terrible, but a preliminary rub with abrasive paper revealed a clean surface without too much effort. The fence and table insert, originally plated, would need more work, as would the bed bars which were pitted on their upper surfaces.

In fact rust was more or less limited to the upward-facing surfaces even of moving parts, suggesting that the saw had deteriorated while standing unused in a damp environment. Severe condensation draws down from the air, vertical and downward-facing surfaces attracting moisture to a much lesser extent. Because of this, even a newspaper laid over a machine will drastically reduce condensation – worth remembering.

Plan ahead
After the oil had done its work the machine came apart easily. Removing the badly rusted sawblade revealed a gleaming arbor, confirming that deterioration had occurred while in storage and that mechanical condition should be good.

Had I intended just to get the thing working, very little work would be needed – new drive belts, cleaning and greasing moving parts, rust treatment and new wiring – but in the interests of research I planned to recondition it, and to fit a new single-phase motor, *see panel*.

> ## "To avoid finding yourself staring helplessly at a heap of unidentifiable bits of metal later on, as soon as it is removed put each group of parts into a labelled bag or envelope"

BELOW LEFT: Before...

ABOVE: ... and after

BELOW: A depressing sight – upward-facing surfaces rusted by drawn-down condensation

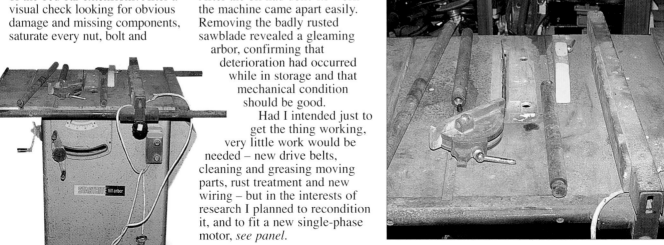

SECRET WEAPON

My metalworking equipment and skills are
barely existent, and at certain key points in
this project I would have been lost without
the help of engineering ace Jack Goodsell –
yes, Alan's dad – who dealt with the
sheared stud and sundry other bits of
intractable metal with cheerful aplomb.
My thanks.

rust, but while easily applied to small components it is no fun to brush onto large areas.

Painting the handles and mitre-guide lulled me into complacency, but I realised I was in trouble about half way through the first side of the cabinet. I persevered but the result is disappointing – next time it's the spraygun for me.

A couple of chromed parts looked scruffy; these were sent to Albion Plating, 01403 710163, who returned them in better than new condition.

Treating the rust on bare metal, non-mechanical surfaces like the table and bed bars was straight-forward but messy; I simply hand-sanded them with aluminium oxide abrasive paper.

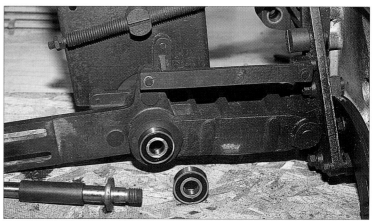

This meant a complete strip-down. In the thrill of dismantling it is easy to forget about reassembly, but to avoid finding yourself staring helplessly at a heap of unidentifiable bits of metal later on, as soon as it is removed put each group of parts into a labelled bag or envelope.

Sub-assemblies such as a handle, its nut, washer, collar and bearing should be kept together, and sketches made of any assembly which won't be obvious later.

Paint and plating

The cabinet, fence bar and table insert went off to be shot-blasted – with hindsight I should have sent the bed bars as well.

At the time I intended to spray the cabinet, in which case having it blasted and primed was a good plan, but for one reason or another I ended up brush-painting it with Hammerite.

Now this paint is a good, rust-treating and durable finish which could have been applied over the old paint after wire-brushing any

TOP: **Arbor bearing's number is engraved on rim, but if illegible then
diameters and thickness will enable identification**

ABOVE: **Drift bearings out of their seats with progressive pull or pressure**

BELOW: **G clamp and wooden blocks good for pressing bearings in**

This removes rust without making much of a dent in sound metal – fine for these components, although more critical machined tables such as those of a planer might need surface-grinding by an engineering firm to maintain or restore flatness.

After sanding, the bare metal was brushed with an automotive rust treatment to keep the demon metal worm at bay.

Rusty mechanical components must be wire-brushed with oil as a lubricant, because an abrasive will alter tolerances with potentially disastrous results; the wire brush is also useful for cleaning threads clogged with compacted wood dust.

Bearings

Some parts – bearings, drive belts and universal joints – may be regarded as consumable, and should be replaced while the saw is dismantled and easy to work on. Don't worry that the machine is obsolete; these are standard engineering parts which are easily available.

So, although the arbor's bearings felt OK, they were dealt with. Bearings are fitted into seats of exact diameter so 'drifting' them out must be done with a steady pressure or pull – not pounding with a hammer!

LEFT: Make sure that any retaining circlips are re-fitted

BELOW LEFT: Typical universal joint failure – this one has been previously repaired with a galvanised nail

BELOW: Failed original joint and HPC's much stronger replacement

JUST A PHASE

ABOVE: Single phase 3HP motor is physically larger than three phase 2HP original, but fits in perfectly

I thought that converting this 2hp, three-phase machine to 1.5hp, single-phase operation by replacing the motor 'should be child's play'.

Well, swapping the motors was easy enough, but finding one was a little trickier.

First I phoned a 'major supplier' who told me that it is impossible to make a single-phase motor larger than 1hp. Since this is clearly nonsense, I gave up with them and tried Brook Crompton, makers of the Gryphon motors fitted to Startrites as original equipment. After being referred to three of their regional offices, their Doncaster office sent me a catalogue of their off-the-shelf motors, one of which would just about do the job.

However, I was lucky enough to find an original single-phase Gryphon motor, still boxed and sealed. I fitted a 3hp example, with a starter switch from Axminster Power Tool Centre.

If I were starting again, though, I would not pursue this method of phase conversion unless I had a second-hand motor lined up. One of Axminster's phase converters is not much dearer, at £317.25, than a new motor and switch.

"Bearings are fitted into seats of exact diameter so 'drifting' them out must be done with a steady pressure or pull – not pounding with a hammer!"

Unless you have a set of engineering pullers, this means cobbling together studding or a coachbolt and oversize washers until you can un-seat the bearing progressively with the turn of a nut.

Once out, the bearings can be identified by the number on their rim, *see photo*. If these are illegible, a good bearing supplier will be able to identify them from their internal and external diameters, thickness and the purpose for which they are used.

Re-fitting bearings is a reverse of removal; here, a G cramp is ideal for pressing them into their seats, *see photos*.

Universal joints

The universal joints fitted to Startrite saws are feeble devices and, although only one had failed, both were to be uprated. Startrite themselves supply a heavier replacement which used to be about £20 each – they've gone up a bit

in the last four years, though, their current price being £66.27.

Two of those would cost more than the saw did, so I turned to HPC Drives whose catalogue contains thousands of useful bits and pieces. One of their UJs was almost perfect, requiring only one modification which HPC carried out in time to deliver two within a week. A good firm, with very helpful technical people.

The cost? Including modification and VAT, £21.62 each, which is more like it.

Together again

Thanks to the labelling mentioned earlier, reassembly was straightforward. Everything was oiled as it went back, and each mechanical assembly was tested before moving on to the next.

All of the usual pre-flight checks were made, then the big

moment – switching on. I'm pleased to report that the machine started without incident and ran smoothly with a gentle hum.

Was it worth it? I wouldn't recommend undertaking quite as extensive a reconditioning as I did unless you have some spare time, as more hours than I care to add up went into it – but to achieve a usable machine needn't have taken as long, and normally it would be in better condition when bought.

As it is, the cost of the project was £560 including VAT, *see panel*, which isn't bad for a secondhand cast-iron sawbench, but for an example with a new motor and switchgear, belts, bearings and universal joints I consider it a good deal.

Only one problem – does anyone have a cross-cut table they don't need?

COSTS AND SUPPLIERS

Cost of machine	£146.88	G&M Tools, tel 01903 892510
Shot blasting and priming	£58.75	Carlton Spray Finishes Ltd, tel 01444 246897
500ml Hammerite	£8.75	
Two drive belts	£12.55	Redhill Bearings, tel 01444 400900
Two arbor bearings	£17.13	Redhill Bearings
Two universal joints	£43.24	HPC Drives Ltd, tel 01246 455500
Motor	£235	
Switch	£37.69	APTC, tel 01297 33656

Superior shooting

● BOB WEARING has spent a lifetime teaching woodwork and furniture design. A respected author on the subjects, his titles include The Essential Woodworker, The Resourceful Woodworker and Hand Tools for Woodworkers, all published by Batsford. He also contributes to F&C's new sister publication The Router.

ASK ABOUT the use of a shooting board, particularly in communal workshops, and the reply is likely to be on the lines of: "We've got one somewhere, but we don't get on with it."

On further questioning, the offending jig will be dragged out covered with several years of dust, from some dark recess.

The stop will probably be out of square and the board itself cut away by canting the plane. These defects can, however, be prevented, and a far better board constructed.

Dimensions of the shooting board should suit the type of work anticipated, the materials available and the size of the plane. Jack or try planes have an advantage.

For those working on a smaller scale, the shooting board may be scaled down for use with a block plane.

Baseboard

Start by making the baseboard. Because solid wood may warp, choose instead multi-ply, MDF or blockboard. Plane an accurate, straight front edge and from it mark and cut two squared ends; the accuracy of these ends is very important.

Screw a strip underneath to be gripped in the vice; this will be useful for some of the constructional stages which follow.

Working from the ends, rout two housings for the end stops; these do not run right through.

Prepare the two end stops and gently thickness them until a snug fit into the housings is obtained – the width depends on the size of the plane to be used. Rout the two screw slots, but leave cutting the small housings until later.

Obtain some 3mm acrylic sheet of any colour, bought as scrap from firms making plastic and illuminated signs – see Yellow Pages – and plane its two long edges. A planer accomplishes this job best, but hand-planing may be substituted.

When the edges are true saw off two strips 20mm (¾in) wide. Use of a hacksaw blade, although slow, saves the bench saws; a fine bandsaw may be used but a circular saw will splinter the material. Sharp edges can be softened with a cabinet scraper.

Drill and countersink one strip and screw it to the baseboard. Gauge its position from the true edge of the baseboard and fix accurately to this line.

The end stops are notched to go over the acrylic runner. They can now be glued and screwed in place. Locate the front end about 1mm

> "The board is made double-ended not so much to accommodate left- and right-handers, but to enable components with a moulded edge to be planed"

(⅜₄in) behind the runner, checking that the angle between the end stop and the runner is an exact 90°.

Upper guide

The innovative upper guide is the anti-canting device. Begin its preparation by drilling the second acrylic strip. The wooden components of the guide can be machined out of hardwood stock, and rebated to take the second acrylic strip. This is then screwed to the two end stops through the top.

The upper guide is secured by two woodscrews which operate through over-sized holes, this arrangement permitting slight adjustment when tested as follows:-

Obtain a small 30in school geometry set square and cut off from the short side so that it will just slide under the upper guide. Hold the plane firmly against the two acrylic runners, then slide in the set square. Adjust the upper guide until the plane fits snugly against the runners, with the sole exactly square to the base. Then fully tighten the screws.

To bring the cutting position nearer to the centre of the blade, thus avoiding the dead corner, prepare a piece of 10mm (⅜in) plywood to fit between the end stops, rebate this to fit over the runner, then screw it to the baseboard.

The purpose of a shooting board is to make the craftsman's life easier. The workshop holding jig – which comes in several varieties – is designed to enable a wooden component to be held accurately at a true right-angle, so that a 90° face can be planed. A finely adjusted plane can be applied to take off delicate shavings, so achieving absolute accuracy.

A simple version – often just two boards sandwiching a veneer – is an essential tool when truing up veneer joints.

The version described by Bob Wearing is easy to use and quick to adjust, so should convert those who have found some other devices too awkward.

Shooting boards come into their own when end-grain has to be planed, overcoming the disadvantages of gripping material in an ordinary vice, when either a scrap piece of wood must be cramped at one end to prevent the plane tearing out, or planing must be done from both directions.

Use of a shooting board provides a faster, easier and more accurate alternative, especially when delicate fitting must be achieved.

Colin Eden-Eadon

board

Bob Wearing explains how to make his special shooting board

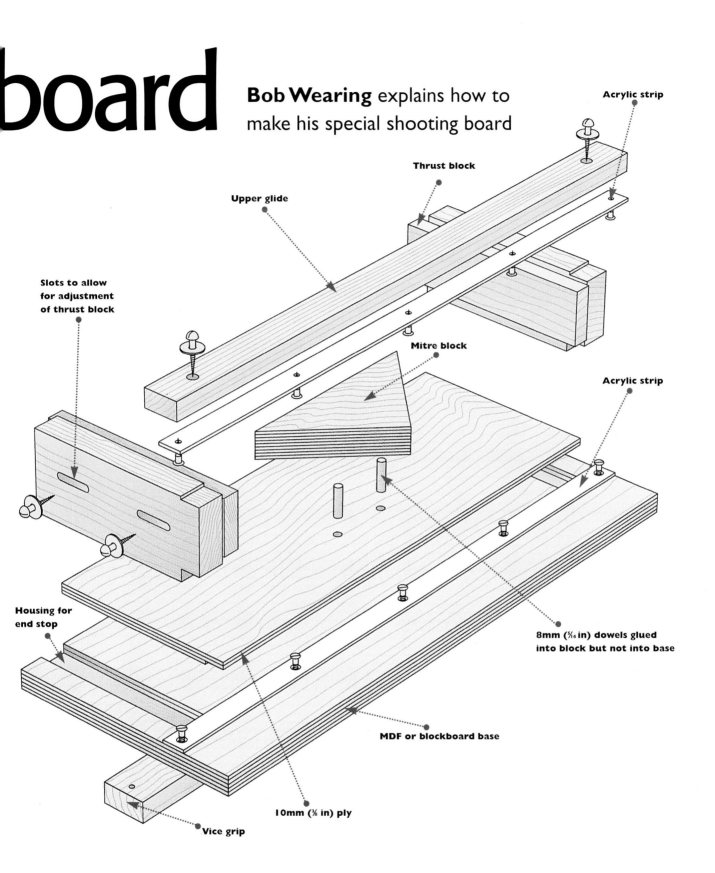

Acrylic strip

Thrust block

Upper glide

Slots to allow
for adjustment
of thrust block

Mitre block

Acrylic strip

Housing for
end stop

8mm (⅝ in) dowels glued
into block but not into base

MDF or blockboard base

10mm (⅜ in) ply

Vice grip

Thrust blocks

Next, prepare the two thrust blocks, allowing enough length in the blocks to accommodate adjustment as necessary. A small bevel must be planed on the edge of the face screwed to the end stops to avoid the end-grain splitting off the thrust blocks in use.

Fix the blocks in place with No. 12 screws and large repair washers. Planing the slightest of tapers on the thrust blocks will bring the end stops into square with the runners, should correction be necessary. The tool can now be fettled, *see panel*, ready for use.

In use

The board is made double-ended not so much to accommodate left- and right-handers, but to enable components with a moulded edge to be planed. In these instances the piece should be planed into the moulding to prevent spelching – the tendency of end-grain to split off at the finish of a stroke – the thrust blocks prevent this occurrence on the square-ended pieces which constitute the majority of work.

As the thrust blocks are eventually over-cut or planed away they can be advanced and trimmed to perfection.

Mitre block

A mitre block accessory is useful for mitring small frames, the width of the frame which can be handled depending on the length of the shooting board; beware, however, of mitring wide frames, since any shrinkage will inevitably open the mitre.

> "Because solid wood may warp, choose instead multi-ply, MDF or blockboard"

Because solid wood may shrink, so rendering the angle inaccurate, the block must be built up from layers of multi-ply.

Plane an accurate 90°, then screw in place. Hold a plane in the working position and check with a large set square that the block is at 45° to the plane.

Two further holes are then drilled through to take two 8mm (⁵⁄₁₆in) dowels. These are glued into the block only so that it can be removed and replaced without loss of accuracy.

Finishing

A coat or two of sanding sealer or varnish adds a bit of dignity to the tool; a large screw-eye for hanging reduces the risk of damage. ▓

JUST THE JOB

A special plane, or at least a particular iron, should be reserved for shooting board work. This should be ground quite straight and square, with no trace of a curve.

Exerting a firm grip, lay the plane in its working position on the vice, then advance the thrust blocks until the plane just catches on them. Secure the screws well, then plane the thrust blocks until there are no more shavings.

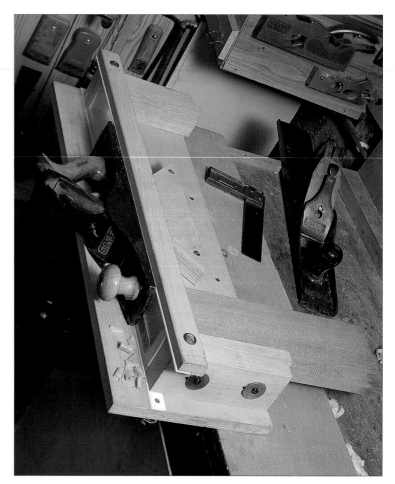

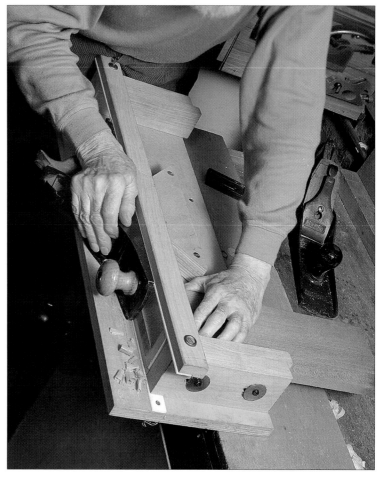

Sharpshooter

Bob Wearing

devises an improved
mitre shooting board

MITRES COME in two forms. The first is used when mitring flat strip, like a picture frame, for example, and can be dealt with by the addition of a mitre block to the shooting board, *(see page 30)*. The second is used when mitring boards for, say, boxes and trays.

These mitres are shot easily and accurately on the board described below. It is an improvement on the traditional 'donkey's ear' shooting board, now seldom made, and the expensive mitre shooting cramp, which, I believe, is no longer manufactured. The cramp was easily damaged and liable to become inaccurate due to shrinkage or swelling.

Construction

Start the construction of this mitre shooting board with a base of 19mm (¾in) MDF or best quality multi-ply, making sure than one long edge and both ends are absolutely true and square to each other. Attach a gripping strip to be held in the vice.

Glue on a strip of plastic laminate, like Formica, and rout a V groove into it, *see diagram*. If a V cutter is not available, rout a 6 by 6mm (¼ by ¼in) groove instead.

Now make the end blocks. These MUST be built up from three layers of 13mm (½in) plywood. If they are made from solid wood, any shrinkage will reduce the angle, producing a combined joint of less than 90°.

Cut the ends at 45°, and rout the two screw slots. Return to the baseboard and rout shallow locating housings.

Form the end blocks and notch them at the mitre end. Screw in place for a trial fit and, if satisfactory, glue and screw.

Support rail

Now prepare the support rail – the innovative component. Angle the working face at 45°, then glue on a strip of plastic laminate, slightly

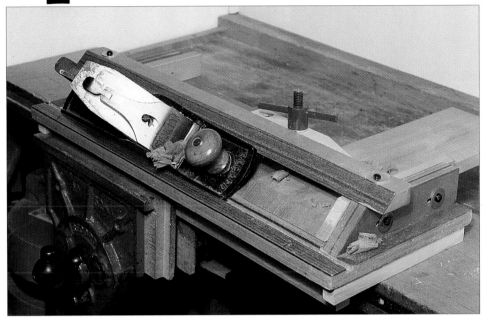

over-wide. When dry, plane or file the excess flush.

Drill over-size holes to permit adjustment, then screw the rail in position, using round head No. 12 screws and large 'repair' washers.

To check for accuracy, saw off a small plastic setsquare to pass under the rail. Lay the plane in position and bring up the setsquare to test. When satisfied, tighten the screws firmly.

Now add a plywood sheet of, say, 13mm (½in) to bring up the workpiece well clear of the corner of the blade. Screw it into place, well countersunk.

Thrust blocks

The final components to make are the two thrust blocks. These prevent spelching – when end-grain bursts out. Make these a comfortable, sliding fit, and mitre the ends.

Screw into place with the screws at the end of the slots furthest from the working face. Hold a plane in place, and, with the aid of a large draughtsman's square, check that the angle between the thrust block and the plane is an exact 90°. Any inaccuracy can be corrected by careful planing of the thrust blocks.

ABOVE: Shooting a mitre – no, it's not that simple, the operator has been removed for clarity

RIGHT: Close up detail

Uses and abuses

Ideally, a special shooting blade, ground and sharpened straight across, should be reserved for the plane. Advance the thrust blocks minutely, then plane each until no further shavings appear. In case of damage or wear, advance the thrust blocks and start again.

These shooting boards are not made double-ended for the convenience of left-handers, but because mouldings must be planed in to avoid spelching.

If the workpiece needs to be cramped, rout a 13mm (½in) groove between the thrust blocks. On a finished board this can be done from underneath.

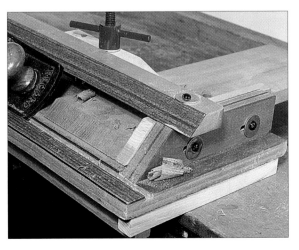

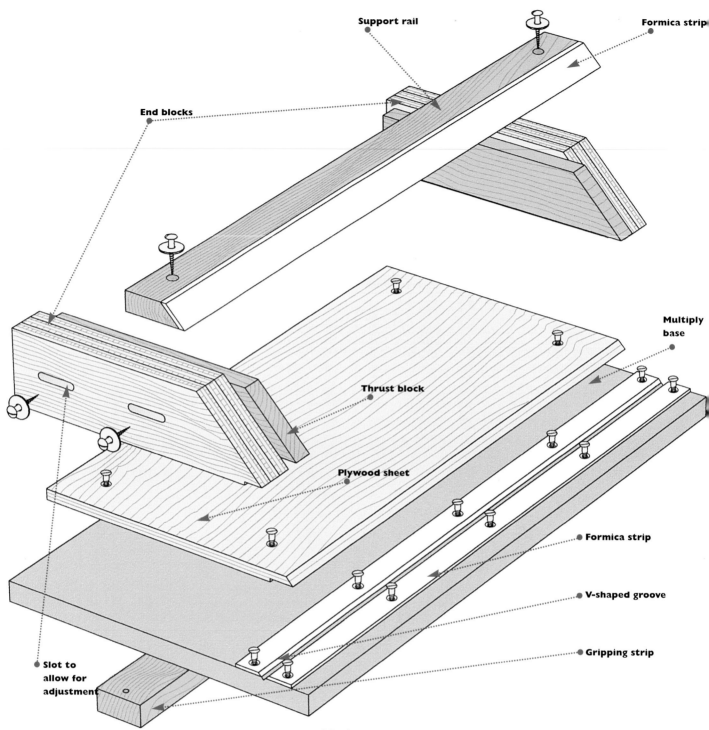

Support rail

Formica strip

End blocks

Multiply base

Thrust block

Plywood sheet

Formica strip

V-shaped groove

Gripping strip

Slot to allow for adjustment

Use either a thin cramp with a wood block behind it, or make a handscrew-like cramp, *see diagram,* allowing room for it by screwing two short wood battens to the underside of the board, and widening the gripping strip accordingly.

Notes on use
The method of use is obvious. For fine work and miniatures, scale down the whole board to accept a block plane. Like the 90° shooting board already described, it is impossible to inflict damage, and the resultant angle is always accurate.

When gluing together mitred boxes, first glue on strips of triangular section softwood to take the cramps. These can be split off easily later, when only a gentle skim over the joint will be necessary.

RIGHT: Mitre shooting board with clamp in place

FAR RIGHT: Clamp is an optional extra

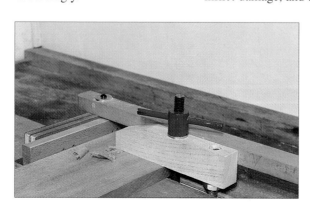

Scotch and mixers

If hide glue were to be introduced today it would, says **Tim Judson**, be dubbed a wonder adhesive

IF THERE WERE ever a holy grail for woodworkers, the search for the perfect adhesive might well be it. For those conditioned to using only proprietary products, the search is liable to be frustrating for, by definition, every adhesive represents a compromise.

Glues such as PVAs, urea formaldehydes, contact adhesives and epoxies all have distinct pros and cons, but at the risk of raising a few eyebrows I am going to put the case for use of a traditional adhesive which has been around for centuries, and which has the facility to extend the range of gluing options for different situations.

For that woodworking staple, Scotch glue, is now often viewed with suspicion and dislike, and is surrounded by a plethora of bad 'craft lore'. If, however, this much maligned glue were to be introduced today, it would likely be hailed as a wonder adhesive.

Used both in furniture-making and for conservation, this glue usually out-performs other alternatives, and its ability to be easily user-modified means that it accounts for about 90% of all my gluing activities.

Animal hides

Scotch glue or, more properly, hide glue in view of its origins, is produced from animal hides which have been soaked in lime for several weeks, then heated to extract the protein material, collagen, from which the glue is formed.

Several extractions are made, each producing a different glue grade. This grading is known as 'gram strength' and refers to the jelly stiffness each type produces when set to room temperature. Gram strengths range from 50 gram gelatines to 500 gram glue for glass chipping.

For woodworking uses, glue strengths range from 135 grams to 379 grams. Different gram strengths produce a range of working characteristics, but most proprietary hide glues can be taken as being a mid-range 251 gram strength, *see panel*.

Typically, the glue is supplied in granule or pearl form – the only difference being that pearls require longer soaking to hydrate fully.

The key to success owes much to accurate preparation: different gram strengths require different amounts of water. The table, *see panel*, shows the ratios of water to glue by weight, but if in doubt calculate at 2:1 as for 251 gram strength.

Hydration

Soak the glue in cold water for at least a couple of hours to fully hydrate the granules before heating to between 60°C and 65.6°C (140° and 150°F). As the table shows, *see panel*, higher gram strengths absorb more water than lower gram strengths, and they set faster. Additionally, they also have great shrinkage factors, so can be used for glass chipping.

This does not pose a problem provided that joints have close mating surfaces with no gaps.

Lower gram strengths require less water, have greater glue film flexibility and less shrinkage, but require longer times for full film strength to set up – two to three days.

Some deviation, with more or less water, is possible from these ratios, but either side can produce problems, either with starved glue lines or non-absorption into wood. To preserve the ratios during use, lids must be kept on glue pots, so preventing evaporation and 'skinning over'.

How glue works

Initially the liquid reaches a 'gel' point as the temperature falls. This gives the 'grab' essential to rub joints.

The second phase is the evaporation of the water, leaving the tightly knit collagen microfibrils as the binding force.

Probably the most problematic aspect of hide glue is its rapid gel point, but this can be slowed by the addition of gel suppressants, either common table salt (*sodium chloride*) or urea. One or the other can be added either to slow the gel time with hot glue, or enough can be mixed in to produce a liquid which, at room temperature, will allow open times of up to 20 minutes.

This will not affect the final glue strength to any real degree. For example, to make a liquid 'cold set' glue, add 3 to 3½ tablespoons of urea – or two of

BELOW:
Ingredients for a wonder glue: pearl and granular glue, fuller's earth for gap-filling, salt to slow setting, and glycerine to plasticise for veneering, plus hot plate and glue pot

salt – to a half cup of hot 135 or 251 gram glue. Use only enough to produce the desired open time, as too much could slightly plasticise the cured film.

I find urea produces a better cold set, despite more being required than salt. Over time, the gel suppressant will slowly degrade the collagen microfibrils, so cold sets have a shelf life of about one year.

Problems with proprietary cold set glues not setting is due to this, so observe the stamped shelf life and date home-made batches. The standard test is to apply a thin film onto a scrap of wood; if it dries to a hard gloss in about an hour, it is still good.

Characteristics

So why bother with different gram strengths? Each grade has varying work characteristics, with excellent shock resistance at above 251 grams, suited to stressed components such as chair joints, and flexibility in lower gram numbers, which are perfect for veneering and cold set applications. All grades exceed the strength of wood when cured.

Hide glue can be plasticised by the addition of glycerine. This is beneficial in veneer work, where veneers move at different rates than, or counter to, solid substrates. For veneering, 2 – 3% glycerine by dry weight is sufficient, but for metal to wood bonds, glycerine can be added up to about 10%.

Most metal inlay bonds fail due to glue inflexibility; use of epoxies are a case in point. To improve the adhesion of the glue, replace 5% of the water with household vinegar (acetic acid) or commercial wallpaper paste.

Garlic juice was traditionally added as a wetting agent – it is a natural surfactant – but for the technically minded, a volatile surfactant such as Surfynol 61, could be used instead; this would subsequently evaporate from the film. Only very small amounts of these need to be added.

"Throw away any that is unused after a couple of days of continuous heating, the cost of the glue being as nothing compared to a glue-up failure"

Dry Scotch glue generally contains mould-inhibiting agents. If mould is found to be a problem, small additions of household bacteriostats will prevent growth. A degree of gap-filling ability can be introduced by adding an inert filler like kaolin/fuller's earth, to reduce film shrinkage, up to a maximum of 30% by weight to dry glue; small quantities of dry pigments can be included to colour gluelines if required.

Heat variant

Heat is another variable with this glue: above 65.6°C (150°F) and the collagen chains will rapidly break down, weakening the adhesive ability. Even maintaining a temperature below 65.6°C will degrade the glue over time, so remove the glue from the heat when not being used and throw away any that is unused after a couple of days of continuous heating, the cost of the glue being as nothing compared to a glue-up failure.

Reducing the glue temperature to around 38°C (100°F) or so will extend the open time and slow collagen breakdown. Storing prepared hide glue in a refrigerator will extend its life; dry glue granules have an indefinite shelf life.

Hide glue is not generally used as an exterior glue, its water reversibility being one of its chief advantages. But for those who wish to do so, hide glue can be made water insoluble by the addition of aluminium sulphate – about ¼% only by ratio – or the dry glue film can be exposed to formaldehyde vapours which will crosslink the glue and make it insoluble.

The usual caveats about health and safety apply, of course – use all necessary protective devices and clothing if handling these chemicals.

Second nature

While the above may seem like a lot of work to those accustomed to using products 'out of the bottle', the methods described are simple and quick to follow, and will soon become second nature.

The advantages of hide glue's versatility greatly outweigh the additional time involved with its preparation. The materials are relatively cheap, with low-tech alternatives possible, such as a variable hot plate and a saucepan of water, or even a coffee mug warmer, replacing a double boiler.

I can only encourage craftspeople to experiment with some of the methods, for the ability of Scotch to be tailored to the specific assembly makes it an invaluable tool to be added to anyone's working repertoire. ■

Suppliers rarely quote, or even know, gram strength specifics, but hide glue in listed gram strengths is available from: Bjorn Industries, 551 King Edward Road, Charlotte, North Carolina 28211, USA.

WATER TO GLUE RATIOS

135g	1¼:1	225g water/180g glue
192g	1⅝:1	292g water/180g glue
251g	2:1	360g water/180g glue
315g	2½:1	450g water/180g glue
379g	2¾:1	495g water/180g glue

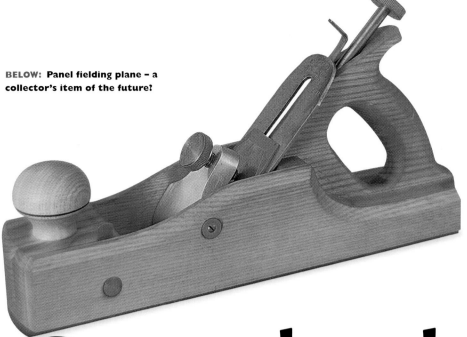

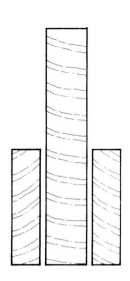

**Handle block
End view**

Steps back in time

Bob Wearing laments the demise of fine adjusting panel fielding planes and demonstrates how to make one

● BOB WEARING has spent a lifetime teaching woodwork and furniture design. A respected author on the subjects, his titles include *The Essential Woodworker, The Resourceful Woodworker* and *Hand Tools for Woodworkers,* all published by Batsford. He also contributes to F&C's new sister publication *The Router.*

WHILE A panel can be bevel-fielded with a jack plane, a far more elegant result is obtained by flat or bevelled step fielding.

Although by no means original, this form of decoration was loved and much used by the Cotswold craftsmen of the Arts & Craft Movement. In some cases these craftsmen used two or even three step fieldings.

This treatment can be attempted using a wide rebate plane or a fillister, but both of these lack the three basic requirements for working other than the most bland of timbers – a fine mouth, a fine adjustment and a cap-iron or 'breaker'.

In the past, these were provided by the wooden 'badger', and some craftsmen improvised by working a rebate along one corner of a jack plane.

A vast improvement was the Stanley, then came Record Carriage Makers' rabbet planes and jack and smoothing plane sizes, the No. 10¹/₂ being a quite sophisticated tool.

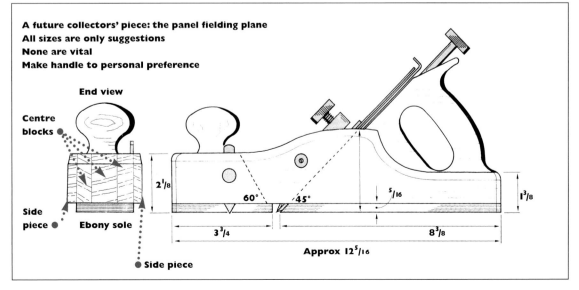

A future collectors' piece: the panel fielding plane
All sizes are only suggestions
None are vital
Make handle to personal preference

End view

Centre blocks ●

Side piece ●   Ebony sole

● Side piece

2¹/₈   60°   45°   ⁵/₁₆   1³/₈

3³/₄   8³/₈

Approx 12⁵/₁₆

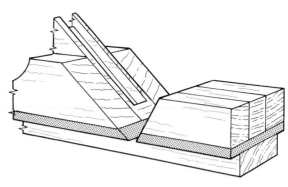

ABOVE: Handle and front block glued or cramped to an assembly board

BELOW: Handle block and front block composition

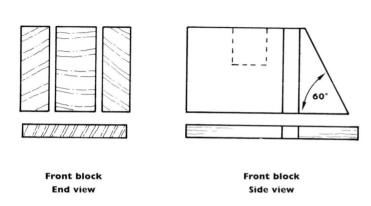

Front block
End view

Front block
Side view

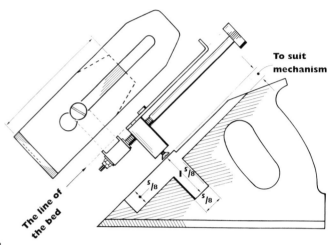

To suit mechanism

The line of the bed

ABOVE: Adjustment mechanism and housing

I can confirm that none of these planes is now made and that there are no plans to reintroduce them. So to produce the step fielding there is but one choice – to make it oneself.

Timber choice

Any good hardwood may be used, so please do not write in to tell me that it must be beech – planes are made in many parts of the world where no beech tree ever grew.

I made this plane from 25mm (1in) quarter-sawn ash.

The body is made in three sections, the bigger thickness at 22mm ($^7/_8$in) to take the handle, so avoiding the necessity to mortice one in.

The thinner sections make up the width to the size of the 50mm (2in) size of the cutter, with a little easing, *see also F&C 6 on making a jack plane.*

Method

Shape the outside rear components, then glue together the three parts. The handle may be roughly sawn to shape. Similarly assemble the front block.

After the glue up, adjust if necessary to give a width about 3mm ($^1/_8$in) greater than the blade width to allow some lateral adjustment. True the bases accurately square to the sides. Saw and plane, or disc sand the bed at 45° and the escapement at 60°.

Glue the harder soles in place. This material can be ebony or

BELOW: Adjustment mechanism components – above left, cylindrical mounting block; below left, sliding block; centre, lateral lever; top right, cap iron screw; below, adjuster rod

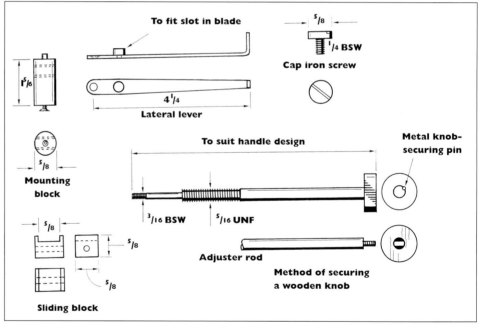

To fit slot in blade

Cap iron screw

$^5/_8$ | $^1/_4$ BSW

Lateral lever 4$^1/_4$

Mounting block $^5/_8$ 1$^5/_6$

Sliding block $^5/_8$ $^5/_8$

To suit handle design

Metal knob-securing pin

$^3/_{16}$ BSW $^5/_{16}$ UNF

Adjuster rod

Method of securing a wooden knob

rosewood and can be bought as guitar fingerboards – for a more economical and less used plane, increase the height by this thickness. Let the soles overlap all round, then plane flush.

To work the housing for the mechanism, modify the moving vice jaw by adding a parallel strip, *see The Router, No. 1,* then grip the workpiece flush with the benchtop.

First, bore the hole for the

cylindrical block then, working from this applied strip, rout the housing, the adjusting spindle and the sliding block.

Mounting blocks

Mount both blocks on assembly board, either by a couple of dabs of glue, with a paper joint, or by cramping. Hold a blade in position to gauge the width of the mouth, leaving this undersize to be opened out later.

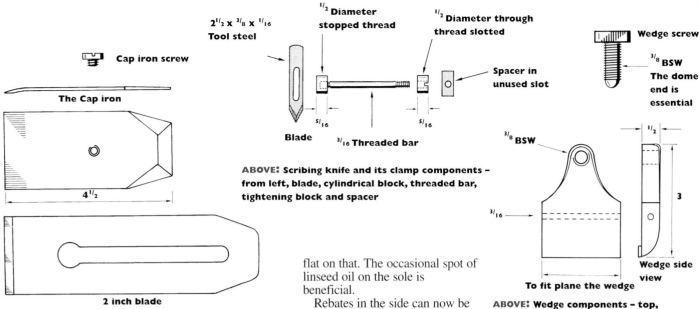

Cap iron screw

The Cap iron

4¹/₂

2¹/₂ × ³/₈ × ¹/₁₆
Tool steel

¹/₂ **Diameter**
stopped thread

¹/₂ **Diameter through**
thread slotted

Spacer in
unused slot

Blade

⁵/₁₆   ⁵/₁₆

³/₁₆ **Threaded bar**

Wedge screw

³/₈ **BSW**
The dome
end is
essential

³/₈ **BSW**

³/₁₆

¹/₂

3

Wedge side
view

To fit plane the wedge

ABOVE: Scribing knife and its clamp components – from left, blade, cylindrical block, threaded bar, tightening block and spacer

ABOVE: Wedge components – top, wedge screw; left, wedge; right, side view of wedge

2 inch blade

ABOVE: Cutter components

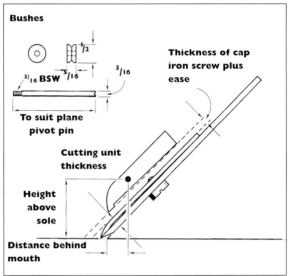

Bushes

¹/₂

³/₁₆ **BSW**   ³/₁₆   ³/₁₆

Thickness of cap iron screw plus ease

To suit plane pivot pin

Cutting unit thickness

Height above sole

Distance behind mouth

ABOVE: Positioning the pivot pin

■ A copy of Bob Wearing's book *The Resourceful Woodworker*, will be awarded for the best photograph of this plane received by the end of January 1998. Send entries to: Fielding Plane, c/o Furniture & Cabinetmaking, 86 High Street, Lewes, East Sussex BN7 1XN.

The housings for the scribing knife can also be cut.

The mainly shaped sides can now be glued in place and held with hand-screws or a number of G-cramps. Clean out any glue from the escapement.

With plenty to grip, now is the most convenient time in which to shape the handle to taste. The sides are best blended into the rear and front blocks using a Carroll drum sander in a drilling machine; use only the end of the drum for the rear block. True up the sole.

Obviously a finely set, sharp planer is ideal. If the sole does not plane well, tape a strip from a glasspaper roll to a piece of 6mm (¹/₄in) plate glass and sand the sole

flat on that. The occasional spot of linseed oil on the sole is beneficial.

Rebates in the side can now be worked to the depth of the applied sole. Ideally, use the router table with a fence; otherwise, use a fillister, a plough plane or gauge, and a small shoulder plane.

Drill for the front knob, then turn it and glue in place.

The ends may now be discretely rounded on a disc sander, then finished by hand-sanding.

Metal components

An engineering lathe is helpful but not essential in making the metal components; hacksaw, files, drills, taps and dies are adequate.

The wedge can be formed from a solid block of aluminium alloy or, if an oversize wood pattern is made, a small local foundry will cast it.

Brass adjusting and clamping screws can be formed in a wood lathe; alternatively, rosewood or ebony knobs can be secured with Araldite. For the assembly of the mechanism, see diagram and photo.

The scribing knife needs a small piece of tool steel. If this is unavailable, it can be sawn from a worn out thin plane iron. Heat to cherry red then allow to cool.

After sawing and filing to shape, heat again, this time quenching in oil or water. Clean off the scale with emery cloth and warm gently until a dark straw colour appears all over. Quench immediately.

If the colour is missed, repeat the sequence. Clean up, sharpen and the knife is ready for use.

Drill, counterbore and fit the knife with its clamp. Generally the knife will be to the right of the plane, with its bevel inwards.

The position of the wedge pivot is critical. It can be drawn out on the plane. Drill just the 3mm (¹/₈in) hole and try it out. A slight error can be corrected in the counterboring for the brass bushes.

Setting up

Now is the time to set up with a sharp cutter and try out the plane, first on a 22mm (⁷/₈in) edge of softwood. Slacken the wedge screw, adjust the cut and tighten. The last movement of the adjusting screw must always be clockwise.

Considerable tightness is not required – just enough to hold the blade against slight sideways pressure from the fingers. Too much tightness will force down the sole behind the mouth, distorting it.

When using the scribing knife across end-grain or difficult long-grain do not set it deep, but use only the minimum depth. Make sure that both the knife and the plane cutter line up with the edge of the sole.

For difficult timber the rule is a sharp cutter, a close cap iron and a fine cut. There is no need generally to plane against the grain. Transfer the scribing knife to the other side and plane in the opposite direction.

Fielding

A wooden fence is essential for the actual fielding, as is a mullet – a grooved offcut from the frame, which is used to test the fit of the panel.

There is no need to soak the plane in linseed oil, as was once common practice. Two or three coats of one-can polyurethane varnish is fine. Note though, this does not dry on rosewood and possibly not on ebony, so keep the sole untreated.

A final point on the actual fielding: the bevel cut will have slightly undercut the upstand. This should be trimmed vertical with a small shoulder plane. ■

S. TYZACK & SON, LTD.   13

CARRIAGE-MAKERS' RABBET PLANES

Nostalgia time – and tools and prices to make a craftsman weep – from S. Tyzack & Son Ltd's 1938 catalogue

On fuming wood

Jeremy Williams explains the intricacies of this ancient process

I N BYGONE, and less hurried times, wood finishing was a leisurely process. Oak and chestnut were darkened in colour by fuming and, whilst it is a slower process than sloshing on some wood dye, it is still as worth doing today as it was then.

Fuming simply changes the colour tone of the wood, and it imparts a warmth you would be hard put to emulate with a dye.

> "Fuming simply changes the colour tone of the wood, and it imparts a warmth you would be hard put to emulate with a dye"

Fuming being carried out in a garden frame

Woods
Oak (*Quercus spp*) and chestnut (*Castanea spp*) are the woods that work best, as they both contain liberal amounts of tannic acid. You may come across other timbers that have the ability to change colour, but only slightly.

Chemical reaction
Fuming is a chemical reaction which takes place when ammonia vapour comes into contact with the tannic acid present in oak and chestnut. It is perfectly possible to apply liquid ammonia directly to the wood and get a reaction, but it is a messy way of doing it.

Materials
You will need some 880 ammonia, some wide shallow dishes such as plastic plant pot pans, and a reasonably airtight 'tent' or large container to place the work in.

The tent can be made from a large plastic bag held upright with garden canes and sealed with tape. Using clear plastic is a good idea because you can see how the fuming is getting on.

I have used a dustbin upside down, and once, the inside of a transit van for a large table – it is usual to do the fuming after assembly.

Preparation
Get everything that you are going to need ready before you start – the ammonia liquid which should be kept in its bottle with the cap on, the plastic dishes or pans, and the container to fume the work in, making sure that this is big enough to take your work and still have some airspace left.

The workpiece needs to be raised off the ground so that the ammonia vapour can circulate. If you just use blocks or bricks you will be left with undarkened stripes where the vapour has not been in contact with the wood. I used a couple of scrap pieces of timber with nails driven through from the underside so that the wood just rested on their tips.

RIGHT: Oak splat to be fumed, shown with ammonia bottle, shallow dish, and supporting nail block

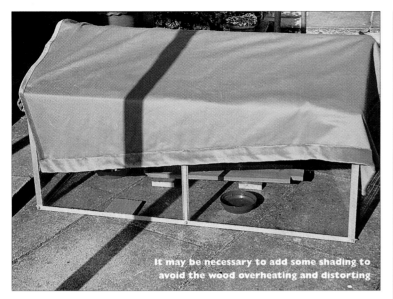

It may be necessary to add some shading to avoid the wood overheating and distorting

"The workpiece needs to be raised off the ground so that the ammonia vapour can circulate"

Ammonia

Pour the ammonia into the dishes – shallow ones are best so that the ammonia comes into contact with plenty of air. The size and number of the dishes will depend on the volume of the air space of the tent you are using.

Ammonia can be dangerous and is toxic – contact with skin and eyes is extremely painful and inhalation can cause nausea and vomiting. It has a particularly adverse effect on the eyes and contact causes permanent damage so do wear safety goggles and use it out of doors.

Reaction time

The process will take about two hours, but if you do leave the wood in the vapour for longer it won't make much difference, as once the ammonia has reacted with the tannic acid near the surface, it does not draw up more from below – instead, the penetration goes in deeper.

Reaction time can depend on two factors – firstly, the temperature of the air is important. When it is cold you tend to get less vaporisation and the fuming takes longer.

Secondly, if the wood is old, there is likely to be less tannic acid present. It is better to work with fresh-cut oak or chestnut, not reclaimed timber.

You can check the reaction time by comparing the colour change with original stock.

After fuming

Sometimes there seems to be a 'cook on' effect once the wood has been removed from the vapour, and darkening may continue for a short period. You can neutralise any ammonia deposits with water, but if you do this you can expect some raising of the grain.

Never flush ammonia into the drainage system, but instead, put it into a container after use for proper disposal.

The colour-change of fumed wood is permanent and will not be subject to any appreciable fading, unless you leave the furniture in direct sunlight. ∎

ABOVE: A simple tent made from a large plastic bag and garden canes

LEFT: See the difference – fumed oak compared with untreated wood

Unlike what happens sometimes with a wood stain, fuming gives a perfect result on endgrain

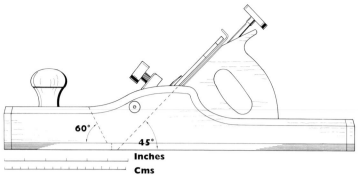

60° 45°

Inches
Cms

ABOVE: Fully adjustable wooden jack plane with ebony sole

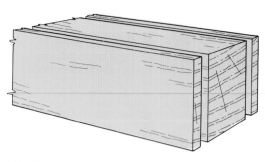

ABOVE: The built-up construction : note the annual rings:-this is the preferred pattern

All right Jack

Bob Wearing describes how to make a wooden jack plane

● BOB WEARING has spent a lifetime teaching woodwork and furniture design. A respected author on the subjects, his books include *The Essential Woodworker, The Resourceful Woodworker and Hand Tools for Woodworkers,* all published by Batsford. He is based in Shropshire.

ALTHOUGH NOT produced in any significant quantity for many years, the wooden jack plane has many firm adherents.

In Roman times woodworkers probably debated the merits of wooden versus metal planes – and more than 1000 years later the argument still goes on: the wooden plane is lighter and has less friction, but a lubricated metal plane is as good; the wooden sole wears hollow, but is easily trued; the metal plane can also be untrue, and truing is laborious.

Other claims have it that the thick blade is less liable to chatter; that the thin blade is

adequate and easier to grind and hone; and fans of wooden planes have no answer to the fact that the metal plane is easily and finely adjustable.

Materials

The construction of a finely adjustable wooden jack plane is well within the capability of any careful craftsman, and can be made entirely by hand or machine.

Before jumping in with both feet, however, make a full-size drawing and apply some careful consideration to the task in hand.

First the blade: thick blades with plenty of life in them can be found; if unsuccessful locally try

Bristol Design, *see panel*. The common jack plane width was 56mm, $2^{1}/4$ in, and a parallel blade – parallel, that is, in thickness not width – is nicer than the more common tapered shape.

Before deciding, consider the grinding facilities available, since grinding these blades is a bigger job.

Thinner blades are easily obtainable in 50mm, 2in and 60mm, $2^{3}/8$ in sizes, the former being more of a school size and perhaps preferred by some female workers (*and by me – Editor*). The 60mm size could be ground down to 56mm, $2^{1}/4$ in by an engineer friend.

Any good, dense hardwood will do for the body, so please don't write in saying beech should be used; planes are made in many parts of the world where no beech tree ever grew, and the plane illustrated was made from dense, old Cuban mahogany, with an ebony sole.

The sole can be part of the basic construction or added from harder material, like ebony or rosewood, available from specialist suppliers as guitar fingerboards; check the width available before ordering. Alternatively, a suitable piece may be sawn out to order by a good timber store, *see panel*.

The body

This comprises two sides, a filling – quarter sawn for stability – and a let-in handle. The annual

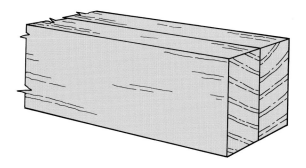

ABOVE: Built-up body block – note the annual ring pattern

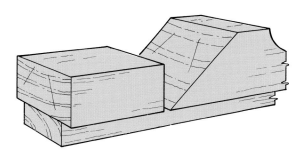

ABOVE: Centre blocks on the building board

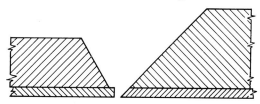

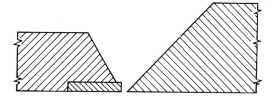

ABOVE: Arranging the mouth – above, the planted sole, below, the solid sole with filler piece

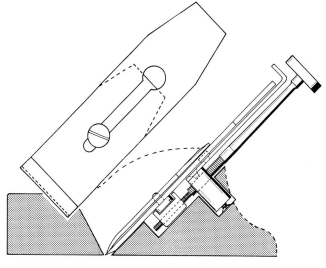

ABOVE: The mechanism in detail

rings, seen from the end, should be as illustrated. The required thickness can, if necessary, be made up from two matching pieces.

Prepare the filling to width and thickness, by machine if possible. Thickness should be 3mm, $^1/_8$in more than the cutter width to permit lateral adjustment, and a fraction more will do no harm.

Saw off the front section at an angle of 60° and the rear at 45°. The rear section can now be bored and routed to accept the mechanism. Both sections may now be mounted on a building board and held by several dabs of glue; the resultant paper joint can be split off with ease later.

Cutting mouth

Do not try to cut the mouth precisely if there is to be no added sole; accuracy is difficult to obtain and over-cutting is all too easy. Instead, arrange a larger mouth, *as shown*, routing a cavity and re-mouthing with the same material after completion. With the blade fitted, the inlaid piece can be adjusted exactly.

If a harder sole is to be added, refer to the drawing to obtain a suitable spacing, erring on the side of too fine a mouth, then gradually ease it back with a thin warding file.

While the glue is drying, prepare the two sides, marking out with a card template and cutting a matching pair from a 25mm, 1in board. Thickness

these to 8mm, $^5/_{16}$in, and glue on with a synthetic resin such as Cascamite or Aerolite, allowing a small overlap. Clean out any glue from the escarpment and plane away the overlap.

Saw out by bandsaw if you have one, or more laboriously by bowsaw. Clean up the shape with a Carroll drum sander in the drilling machine, using the table illustrated.

Split from the baseboard and clean up just the sole; if using an added sole it is glued on at this point.

The handle

Preparation of the handle comes down to personal preference, see drawing for guidance. This shape was also cleaned up with a small Carroll sander, rounded nicely with a wood rasp and wood file, and finished with several grades of glasspaper.

Gauge the socket for the handle, either chopping out with a mortiser or drilling 22mm, $^7/_8$in holes to remove most of the waste, then paring to the lines. Rout the groove for the adjusting screw, then glue into place, removing all traces of extruded glue.

Drill a hole for the cylindrical block, and complete the excavation for the mechanism.

Turn the front handle with a substantial tenon, polish and glue in place.

Making mechanism

The wedge can be made from

metal or wood sawn out of a piece of thick bar material. The aluminium alloy model illustrated was, however, cast from an oversize pattern by a small local foundry. The final shape is obtained by filing, and finished by working through the grades with emery cloth.

Drill the pivot hole, then drill and tap for the clamping screw. By careful measurements, *see illustration*, locate the position on the body of the pivot pin.

The crude solution is simply to

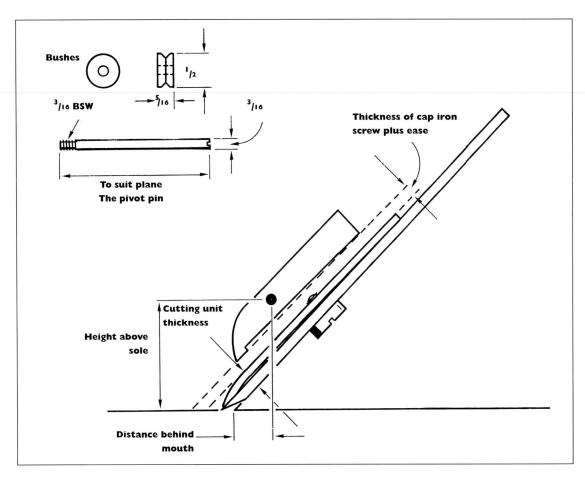

Bushes

$^3/_{16}$ BSW

$^1/_2$

$^5/_{16}$

$^3/_{16}$

To suit plane
The pivot pin

Thickness of cap iron
screw plus ease

Cutting unit
thickness

Height above
sole

Distance behind
mouth

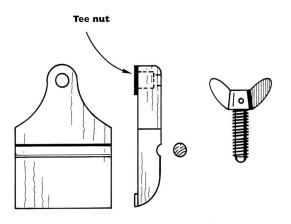

Tee nut

ABOVE: Alternative wedge and screw with tee nut, centre

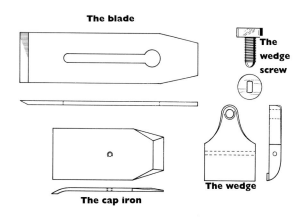

The blade

The wedge
screw

The wedge

The cap iron

ABOVE: Components – clockwise from top left, blade,
wedge screw, wedge and cap iron

drill the body with the pin size, but after a while this hole may elongate. The better method, shown, is to drill larger holes – with a piece of scrap wood inside to prevent bursting through – and fit two brass bushes, one with a clearance hole and the other a threaded hole.

These are glued in place with an epoxy resin like Araldite. Such bushes may be turned in a wood lathe, using a hand tool ground at about 80°.

Cylindrical block

Mild steel rod is the preferred material for the cylindrical block. Turn the little spigot, then drill and tap for the adjusting screw. Two small flats may be filed if the block needs to be glued into place, but this procedure will not be necessary if the fit in the hole is good.

Because the pre-bored hole will not necessarily be to the precise depth required, the height of the mechanism may be adjusted with the small screw at the bottom. If a removable mechanism is intended, grease the block well; however dry the timber, after a while the steel block will rust.

Adjusting lever

Make sure the lateral adjusting lever and boss fit the blade slot well. Position the lever on the block and rivet over the spigot tightly enough to produce a stiffish movement.

Two cut adjusting screws are shown, the top one giving a fine adjustment by differential screw. The easiest way to accomplish this is by drilling and tapping the spindle, then inserting a piece of screwed rod.

Force it in tightly with a pair of locked nuts or turn down and thread the spindle; all the advantage of the fine adjustment will be lost if the fine screw fits sloppily.

The plain shank goes through the sliding block to be held by two locked nuts, the $^5/_{16}$in UNF or 8mm Metric Fine thread for the lower spindle producing a finer adjustment than the Record/Stanley-type planes.

Sliding block

The sliding block can either be built up and silver-soldered or, more tediously, filed from the solid. Again, that engineer friend might mill you a couple of inches from which to saw off the block. This is threaded for the fine

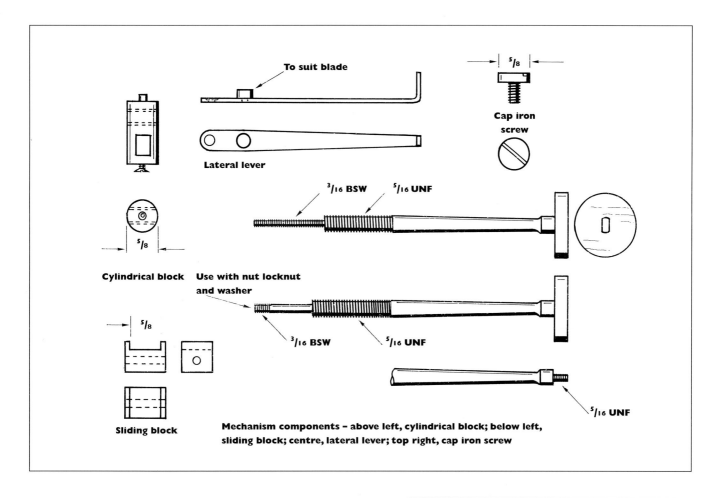

Mechanism components – above left, cylindrical block; below left, sliding block; centre, lateral lever; top right, cap iron screw

(Labels within diagram:) To suit blade • Lateral lever • Cap iron screw • Cylindrical block • Use with nut locknut and washer • Sliding block • ³/₁₆ BSW • ⁵/₁₆ UNF • ⁵/₈

adjustment model and clear-bored for the simpler one.

The wedge screw is simply a piece of bought screwed rod, or even a piece from a screw, but it must have a domed tip which can be filed in a drilling machine or lathe.

If the tip is left flat the turning screw may move the blade sideways.

Knobs option

Of course, that engineer could turn a pair of fine knurled brass knobs, but failing that facility there are two options: wood or hand-turned metal.

The wooden knobs, *shown*, of rosewood or ebony, are turned and bored centrally to fit the spindle and screw which have two considerable flats filed. The knobs are glued on with Araldite, the gaps being well filled. Wipe off the excess from the inside and leave proud on the outside. When thoroughly dry, return them to the lathe and skim over the outside face.

Simplification

For those not wishing to construct the mechanism, the plane can be hammer adjusted by

making a simpler wooden wedge arrangement from a hard, dense wood, *see drawing*. Fit an M8 Tee nut, cut off the screw from M8 screwed rod or from a long screw, dome the end and secure a wing-nut with a pin.

Drill and glue in an 8mm, ⁵/₁₆in dowel in place of the steel pivot bar, and work a matching groove in the wedge.

Fitting blade

If the thicker blade is to be used, make the cap iron from mild steel, *as shown*. The ready-made cap iron is satisfactory for the thin blade, so long as it matches the sliding block.

A little experience will be required to balance the two screws. Slacken the wedge screw before adjusting the cut, then tighten. When reducing the cut the last movement must always be clockwise to ensure that any slack is taken up in the mechanism.

The wedge screw needs to be only tight enough to hold the blade firm against finger pressure; excessive tightening can result in pressure just behind the mouth which can distort the sole.

SUPPLIERS

THICK BLADES can be obtained from Bristol Design, tel 0117 929 1740.
Timber for the sole can be had from
■ *John Boddy's Fine Wood & Tool Store Ltd*, Riverside Sawmills, Boroughbridge, North Yorks, tel 01423 322370, fax 01423 323810,
■ *Alan Holtham*, The Old Stores Turnery, Wistaston Road, Willaston, Nantwich, Cheshire, tel 01270 67010 and *Craft Supplies Limited*, 275 The Mill, Millers Dale, near Buxton, Derbyshire, tel 01298 871636, fax 01298 872263.
Carroll sanding drums are available from
■ Carroll Tools Ltd, 16-18 Factory Lane, Croydon, tel 0181 781 1268, fax 0181 781 11278.
    The taps and dies mentioned can be obtained from most good tool shops; ordering such small items by post can be expensive.

Finishing

This plane does not require old-fashioned soaking in linseed oil. Either apply a conventional oil polish, with a reviver coat every few months, or finish with a satin or matt polyurethane varnish – except for the sole which should have the occasional wipe of linseed oil.

Finally, true the sole, using either a freshly sharpened planer or a succession of finer grades of abrasive papers, taping down to the sawbench table or a piece of plate glass. ▪

Taking the

Bob Wearing on making a jointing board

AT SOME TIME or another the need to widen a surface by edge-jointing will arise. For those without a planer or jointer, or lacking the experience to make a good job of hand-jointing — or simply when time is of the essence — help is at hand in the form of the versatile router.

Basically all that is required is a jointing board. This consists of two boards forming a flat machining bed on which the router and the work sit, with a slot to take the cutter. A separate fence is clamped to the assembly.

The length of the board depends on the size of work contemplated; for width, the dimensions given, *see below*, are generally suitable.

Method of work

Clamp on the first piece to be jointed, true face upwards. If the component is small, *see photo*, hold it with several strips of double-sided tape. This first piece must overhang the central gap by, say, 6mm (¼in) or a little less.

Similarly, fix the second workpiece, true face down, but this time just clear of the gap; its sole purpose, so far, is to keep the router level.

Set up the router without a side fence and fit a good quality TCT straight cutter with a cutting length greater than the thickness of the workpiece; 12.5mm (½in) diameter or greater is quite suitable.

"If there is any unsquareness between router base and cutter, try cramping one workpiece with its true face up and the other with its true face down"

CONSTRUCTION

MDF is coming under increasing criticism on health grounds and may have a tendency to sag in length. Make the edge-jointing board from two pieces of good quality multi-ply or blockboard.

Screw these onto two battens, adding extra battens if a longer board is needed and leaving a space between them of about 25mm (1in). Add a lengthwise batten to act as a gripping piece in the vice. Finally, make a fence.

easy route

LEFT: **Board set up for second cut**

Clamp on the fence so that the router, when its baseplate is run along it, will take a cut no greater than 3mm (⅛in), preferably less. Switch on and traverse from right to left.

Running a pencil line along the edge is helpful; even if the router should drift away from the fence, leaving pencil marks, no harm is done. Have another go and all will be well.

Second cut

The first workpiece and the fence must not be disturbed. Release the uncut piece and secure it over the gap. To obtain a convenient gap between the two components, turn the router bit so that the actual cutting edges are clear of the wood, then move in the second piece until it touches the cutter at both ends and fix it firmly.

Again, traverse the router along the fence, this time from left to right. The joint is now complete. In the event of the router drifting away from the fence, move the workpiece in a little more and traverse the router again.

Note that the cut can only be made at full depth; two cuts with a short router cutter will not work.

If there is any unsquareness between router base and cutter, try clamping one workpiece with its true face up and the other with its true face down. To exaggerate, this action will cut one board at 91° and the other at 89°, the combination being 180°, i.e. flat.

Variation

A router with a circular baseplate run along a curved fence could be used in this way to create an interesting joint, particularly when contrasting woods or components with very differing grain patterns are jointed. ■

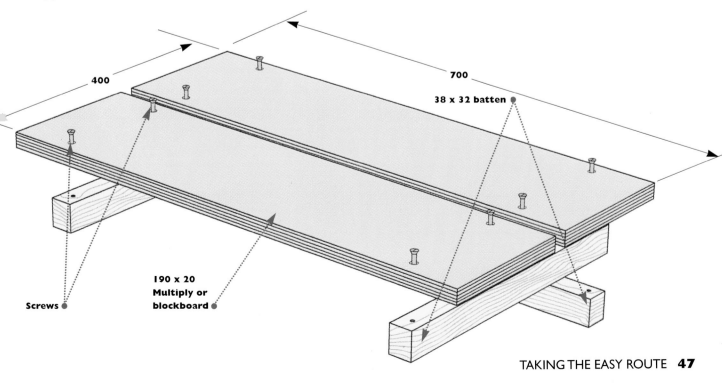

400

700

38 x 32 batten

190 x 20
Multiply or
blockboard

Screws

Tailor-made s

ABOVE: The inlay thicknesser

MOST CABINETMAKERS, restorers and turners will, from time to time, use inlay stringing. It can, of course, be bought ready-made, but it is much more convenient to make it yourself. Workshop-made stringing can be produced in any type of wood and at the exact size that you need – with the added advantage that it is much easier to produce stringing to suit a previously worked groove than it is to file up a cutter to suit bought-in stringing.

With all this in mind I set out to make a tool that would do the job – and here it is. The metal components have been reduced to a minimum and the woodwork is quite straightforward.

"With all this in mind I set out to make a tool that would do the job – and here it is"

"It is much easier to produce stringing to suit a previously worked groove than it is to file up a cutter to suit bought-in stringing"

Construction
Start by cutting out a template for the sides from substantial card and prick through the centres for the five holes. Prepare two pieces for the sides and tape them together

Thicknessing rosewood stringing

tringing

Bob Wearing
reveals how to make
an inlay thicknesser

LEFT: View from the rear

with the template on top. Drill through the two small holes at 1.5mm (¹⁄₁₆in) and then draw round the template with a fine ball-point.

Remove the template and tap in two panel pins, leaving a slight projection for their removal. Saw the sides to shape by bandsaw, jigsaw or coping saw and then true-up the shape. I found that my Carroll drum sander, used in the drilling machine, worked well for this.

Drill the pivot holes and the holes for securing the bridge piece. Separate the two components and counter-sink these screw holes. Remember that there is a left and a right-hand piece.

Prepare the base and the rising table to an accurate width of 51.5mm (2¹⁄₁₆in). Lightly pin each side in position, using the existing holes. Then remove and glue them in place, using 13mm (½in) brass panel pins to locate accurately. Cramp and leave to dry thoroughly. Skim over the bottom and screw

on a strong block for gripping in the vice.

Drill a shallow cavity with a ¾in bit, and then drill through at 8mm (⁵⁄₁₆in). Pull a M6 tee-nut into this using a bolt, washer and drilled wood block. Do not hammer in the tee-nuts as they invariably go in askew.

Rising table

Now take a shaving from the edge of the rising table so that it moves freely in the body. Lay on a small off-cut of 3mm (⅛in) plywood or hardboard at each end and hold the table in place with a cramp. In this position insert the pivot screws. These are 25mm (1in) No.6, giving

LEFT: Blade fixing – rear view

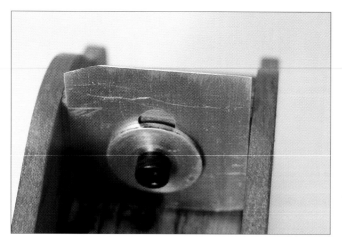

ABOVE LEFT: Blade fixing – front view

ABOVE RIGHT: sawing jig for cutting inlay by hand

an adequate parallel length to act as the pivot.

Prepare a small plywood template at 75° to help locate the bridge piece. Now make the bridge piece to size and obtain a perfect length fit by using a disc sander or a shooting board. Gauge a centre line on each end. Place the bridge in position, using the template to obtain the angle exactly. Tap in 19mm (¾in) No.6 brass woodscrews to mark the position – these can be adjusted if necessary, to be on the centre line. Drill pilot holes. Before fixing, drill a 19mm (¾in) cavity and then go through at 8mm (⁵⁄₁₆in). Pull in an 6mm tee-nut.

Oiling

This is a convenient time to give the tool one or two coats of oil. When dry and rubbed down, screw in the bridge and refit the rising table. If preferred, the bridge screws can be removed, one at a time, to be replaced by glued-in dowels. Slip in the blade and secure it with the large washer and a 25mm by M6 socket screw. The adjusting screw can also be inserted. Add to this a wing-nut to clamp the screw when a number of identical stringings are being produced.

Blade-sharpening

Hone the blade as you would a plane

cutter or a chisel but maintaining the ground angle of 45°. Do not omit the curved feed-in. Flatten the back and repeat on the other ground edge. Lay the blade flat on the bench top and burnish the flat side.

Now grip the blade in a metalwork vice and burnish with only a few heavy strokes. Start at 45° and end at about 15° to the horizontal, thus forming a microscopic hook. Repeat on the other edge. Place in the tool, protecting the exposed cutting edge with a piece sawn from a plastic spine sold by stationers for holding papers together.

Re-sharpening a blade

Lay flat on the bench and with a

PREPARING THE STRIP

Make a false table from wood, saw a slot in it and screw or cramp it to the bandsaw table – a fine blade is recommended. Make a slotted fence and fix it to the table with two M6 countersunk screws in threaded holes, wingnuts and large washers.

Adjust the fence to produce just over the size required. Feed in the material slowly and carefully, making sure that it does not stray from the fence. In some cases the material can be sawn to both width and thickness on one setting.

When the stock to be sawn is narrow, a spring finger is an advantage. Make the spring from say 13 by 3mm (½ by ⅛in) straight-grained ash, and glue it to a drilled block. This is also held by screw, wing-nut and washer. Apply just enough pressure to hold the workpiece firmly to the fence.

Lacking a bandsaw, the stringing can be cut with a fine tenon saw. Prepare a table – ideally 250 by 100 by 19mm (10 by 4 by ¾in) – and glue below it a block to be gripped in the vice. Saw a long slot to take the blade and construct a fence as already described.

Saw in the slot, at about 30°, feeding the material through.

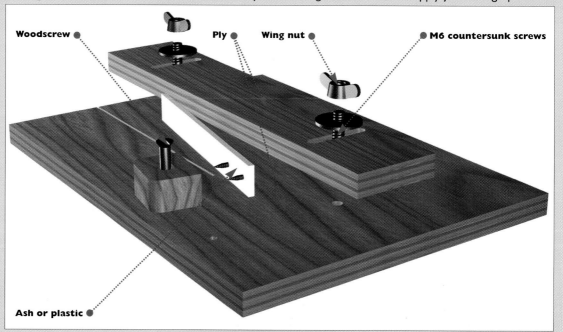

Woodscrew ● Ply ● Wing nut ● ● M6 countersunk screws

Ash or plastic ●

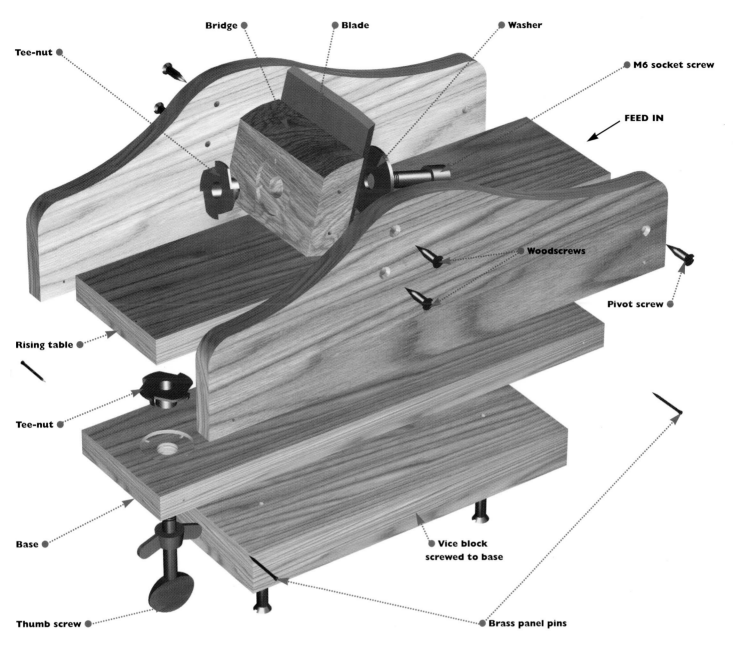

Tee-nut ●

Bridge ●   ● Blade   ● Washer

● M6 socket screw

FEED IN

Woodscrews

Pivot screw ●

Rising table ●

Tee-nut ●

Base ●

Vice block
screwed to base

Thumb screw ●

● Brass panel pins

large flat slip-stone remove all traces
of the old hook. Grip in a metalwork
vice and file a bevel at 45°. Make
sure that the edge is straight and
preserve the feed-in corner. Stone
off any wire edge. Now proceed as
described for a new blade.

Setting up blade
Raise the table to give a gap of about
6mm (¼in). Temporarily fit the blade.
The sharpening bevel must be on the
outside, that is, the furthest side

SHARPENING

To sharpen your inlay thicknesser
you will need a good burnisher.
Don't be tempted to use a
screwdriver because they are too
soft and once they are grooved
they will not burnish well.

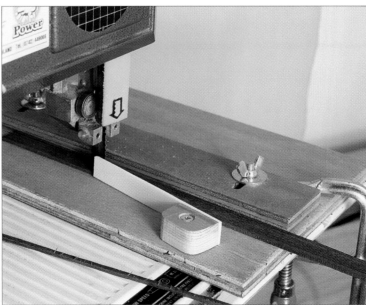

**LEFT: Cutting the
inlay on the
bandsaw**

ABOVE: The hardware from Vanguard Tools

from the bridge. Slacken the clamp screw momentarily to allow the blade to drop to the table and firmly clamp. By this means the blade always remains truly parallel to the table. Lower the table to just permit the entry of the sawn strip under the main part of the blade. Raise the table slightly and lock with the wing-nut if a number of strips are to be thicknessed. Insert a strip through the feed-in gap, either from the front or from the rear, it does not matter which. Grip with a pair of pliers and pull both forward and to the right, that is, to the business part of the cutter. Reverse the strip and pull through again to complete the cut. Do not attempt to take a heavy cut at the start, since the material that is straight from the saw will not be true.

Raise the table slightly and repeat. If several pieces are being thicknessed, do not forget to lock the adjusting screw with the wing-nut after each adjustment. Continue in this manner until the stringing produced is a tight fit in its groove. Try to finish with a really fine cut. Plan carefully the initial setting of the blade so as not to run out of adjustment before the required thickness has been obtained. ■

BELOW LEFT: Inlay thicknesser side view

BELOW RIGHT: End view from right

EUREKA

I discovered that lute and guitar-makers improvised a device for making inlay stringings by cramping a cabinet scraper to an angled block. My first attempt to make something similar was by way of cramping a blade to two angled strips, housed into a block. The next step, influenced by the Record and Stanley scraper plane, was to use a cutting edge of 45° rather than the 90° of the cabinet scraper. All these early models worked tolerably well but adjustment was tedious and very much hit or miss.

The metal spokeshave gave the next inspiration. Basically, a block with a slot cut from its lower edge was housed into the bed at about 70°. This was drilled to take two pieces of 1BA screwed rod, the size in the spokeshave. A round-head woodscrew was fitted centrally, so the tool could now accept all the spokeshave components such as the blade, wedge, clamping screw and two adjusting screws. All that was needed was to grind the edge to 45° and grind away an entry gap.

I was operating a small foundry at my college at the time I was working on this and so the job translated into metal, leaving just the spokeshave parts remaining.

> ## "Unlike Archimedes who had his great idea in the bath, I hit on the breakthrough on a long and dreary coach journey to Austria"

The tool proved to be popular and I considered industrial production. The casting and the woodwork presented no problem but the difficulty lay in buying the parts in bulk – retail prices made the project impossible and there, it seemed, the matter ended.

But, unlike Archimedes who had his great idea in the bath, I hit on the breakthrough on a long and dreary coach journey to Austria. On a planing machine the cutters do not rise and fall, the table does – so why not an inlay thicknesser that works on the same principal?

FACTS AND FIGURES

Metal components for inlay thicknesser	£11.75 inc VAT and p&p
Burnisher	£4.65 inc VAT and p&p

●Available from: **Vanguard Cutting Tools Ltd**, 102 Harvest Lane, Sheffield S3 8EG tel: 0114 2737677

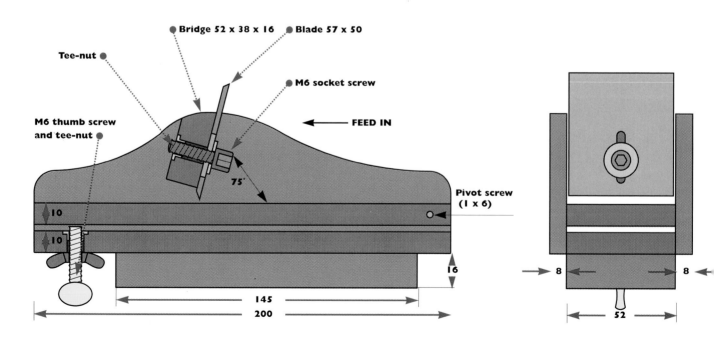

Good as new

Tuning up your planer thicknesser can make all the difference to the quality of cut you achieve

Bill Cain demonstrates tuning-up a planer thicknesser using his Kity 636 as an example

● **BILL CAIN**
underwent an engineering apprenticeship embracing general and machine fitting and toolmaking. He retired early from the Aerospace industry and now spends much of his time writing, and enjoying woodworking and related metalworking in his home workshop

THERE IS an old saying in engineering – 'If it's not broke don't fix it' – and believe me it is a wise maxim! Having said that, any machinery, especially the rotating type, requires regular routine oil-can maintenance, and after a few years of use you may need to go a little deeper and give it a tune-up to restore it to its original performance.

If a machine is out of tune or the knives are not kept razor sharp and correctly ground, then the loads on the machine go up, vibration sets in, machine fixing screws loosen, and

> "Wear and tear plays the major role in this process and eventually 'time-out' is needed to get everything back in line"

the result is poor performance, inaccuracy, and poor quality of finish. Wear and tear play the major role in this process and eventually 'time-out' is needed to get everything back in line.

Tuning-up

My Kity 636 planer thicknesser is quite a few years old now and has had hard use over the past couple of years – and had reached the point where something really had to be done.

Although the work I undertook is specific to the Kity 636, the basic engineering principals employed are similar for many other makes and models of machine. The work stops short of a full overhaul and should be within the scope of woodworkers with a feeling for machines.

KITY 636

The Kity 636 is a good quality, robust machine with, overall, I metre of cast aluminium surfacing tables and fabricated steel frame, thicknesser table, and fence.

The single 1.5hp, 3000rpm fan-cooled induction motor is controlled via an NVR switch – whilst the 7000rpm twin knife cutter-block and 2-speed feed thicknesser is driven by a combination of belts and chain, and runs timber through at 6.5 or 9 metres a minute.

Guarding is simple and effective in sheet steel and cast aluminium.

RIGHT: The Kity 636 – a stalwart of many small workshops

Step 1 Access and inspection

Fully isolate the mains supply to the machine, clean the machine well and remove the cutter knives, their cutter-block locking-bars, and the two small springs that sit below each of the knives. Mark each knife locking-bar to ensure that it is returned to its original location when re-assembled. Remove the fence and the pantograph-style cutter guard.

Working from the rear drive side of the machine, remove the guards. Then mark the direction of travel on the drive belts so that they can be re-fitted in the original direction.

Next, remove the belts. Inspect them for damage and wear and, if you are in any doubt, replace them with new. If the belts are fine, remove any glaze from the working face by a light rub with abrasive paper.

The next step is to inspect the condition of all the drive pulleys for flats caused by the belt slip. Clean up the working faces – note that the drive faces are not flat but have a slight 'crown'. If flats are evident then replace them. Alternatively, if you have access to a lathe they can be trued-up by taking the very lightest of cuts.

Now clean the drive train and inspect, in situ, the condition of the cutter-drive chain, gears and tensioning pulleys. Ensure that the springs of these latter items are doing their job and that the thicknesser belt idler pulley and chain idler sprocket are both free to rotate.

Next, check and tighten the screws, securing the bottom chain drive sprocket to the large nylon or plastic gear.

Finally tighten the nuts securing the thicknesser's main drive pulley and gear to the machine side frame, and the nuts securing the cutter-block bearing housings.

Step 2 Chain

Lay the machine over, operating side face down on some padding, clean and inspect the condition of the thicknesser bed rise and fall drive-chain which is located in the bottom of the machine, and its tensioning and idler gear. If necessary, slacken the idler, re-tension the chain and tighten its fixing – note that the chain must not be taut but free to travel with no sign of binding. Then grease the chain and oil all the bearings.

"The work stops short of a full overhaul and should be within the scope of woodworkers with a feeling for machines"

ABOVE LEFT: Remember to mark each drive-belt's direction before you remove it

ABOVE: Check the drive pulleys for flats and wear

TOOLS

The tools that you will need are:
● 10mm and 13mm spanners and sockets
● a straight edge
● feeler gauges
● a dial test indicator (DTI) and stand/magnetic block
● a No 2 Pozidrive screwdriver
● a spirit level
● a soft face hammer
● pliers or grips

A DTI is not a measuring tool in the true sense, it is a precision comparator and its role is to gauge and display plus and minus deviations from an established datum to a secondary, or working, face. The DTI can take a variety of forms and be calibrated in metric or imperial increments. It is still possible to do some good work even if you do not have a DTI

BELOW: Dial test indicators can be found second-hand at little cost

The rise and fall chain is checked, tightened and cleaned

Step 3 Table

Now with the machine sitting on its base, raise the out-feed table into the thicknesser mode and check that the table height adjuster moves the table freely up and down as intended.

Removal of the out-feed table can be done by gripping the operating spindle of the adjustment mechanism and unscrewing the knob, then removing the four stiff-nuts securing the table to its slides.

Mark the rectangular pressure pad washers to ensure that they are returned to their original location or direction on re-assembly. Now lift and slide the table free.

Clean down, and ensure that the table adjustment screw is well lubricated and moves freely through its full range of travel. Inspect the table V-slides and ensure that there are no burrs or the like – mine had been over-tightened and poorly adjusted at some time and there were high spots evident that caused binding and poor contact in the slides.

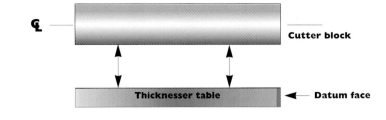

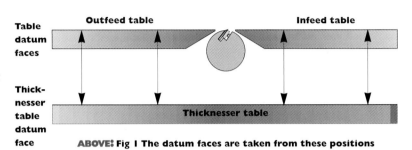

ABOVE: Fig 1 The datum faces are taken from these positions

Now clean this area and ensure that all the anti-kickback fingers are free to rotate. Give the thicknesser drive rollers a good clean and remove any burrs from the out-feed roller.

Check the cutter block bearings for play.

Next, clean all the residues and burrs from the face of the thicknessing table and the cutter block including the knife slot and rotating face.

Step 4 Setting datums

You are now at the stage where you can start to check-out and adjust the basic setting datums for what are, after all,

the key elements of the machine. Firstly, there is the cutter-block relative to the thicknesser table – the two must be parallel to one another if you are to achieve accurate thicknessing. Secondly, there is the out-feed table relative to both the cutter block and the thicknesser table – again, these must be parallel since it is from this out-feed table that the knives are set. Finally, there is the in-feed table relative to the out, for accurate surfacing.

Take it slowly from now on, only moving one item at a time and in small increments.

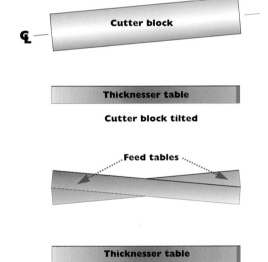

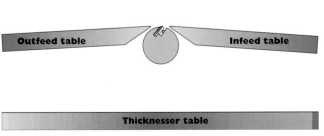

ABOVE: Fig 2 Some of the possible problems that need to be corrected are exaggerated here to show them clearly

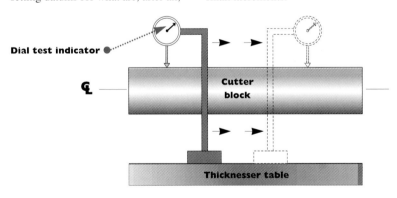

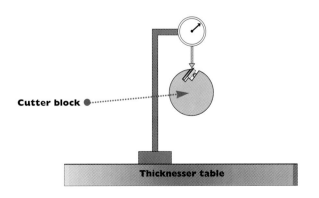

ABOVE: Fig 3 Dial test indicator set up – a similar procedure is used for feed tables

The DTI is set up on the cutter-block and carefully checked

Step 5 Setting cutter-block

At the drive-end, gauge from the thicknesser table face to the top face of the cutter-block, its point of maximum diameter, which is top dead centre. Zero the DTI at the point where the reading changes from plus to minus and record the small rev counter reading – this is very important because if you don't, it is easy to end up with a very distorted reading and setting!

Having zeroed the clock, carefully move it to the operating end of the cutter-block – note the clock and rev-counter readings – the difference between what it now reads and the first set of readings taken from the drive-end, will establish the cutter block alignment and run-out – relative to the thicknesser-table face being used as the master datum.

Any adjustments necessary can be achieved by backing-off the cutter-block bearing housing fixings on the operating side where access is better and, with a soft face hammer, applying a light tap to the housing in the required direction. Pinch up the nuts and repeat the process using the

DTI until you get it right. Tighten the fixings and take a further set of readings to ensure nothing has moved.

Try to obtain the least possible run-out over the 250mm (10in) length of the cutter-block – I managed to get within approximately 0.025mm (0.001in) after adjustment.

The cutter-block to the thicknesser table master datum is now set, and it is from this that all further table and knife settings are to be established, so it is well worth a bit of time and effort to get it right.

> "The Kity 636 has cast aluminium tables, and some degree of wear to the table faces is likely to be evident – at least it was on mine!"

Step 6 Setting-out table

I consider it best to use the far sides and edges of the tables as gauging points, as these will not have seen so much wear as the centre section of the tables.

With the machine standing on a good firm surface, set it level by use of a spirit level over the length and width of the thicknesser table – packers under the machine case will help. Once levelled, transfer the spirit level to the out-feed table, gauging through each of the suggested gauging points.

Adjustment can be achieved by slacking the table-slide's fixings and very gently tapping the slide blocks to achieve a level table.

TOP AND ABOVE: A spirit level is used to set the length and width of the out-feed table

BELOW: Fig 4 Suggested gauging points

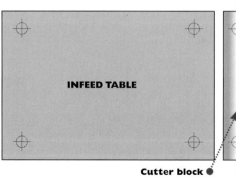

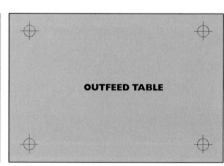

INFEED TABLE

OUTFEED TABLE

Cutter block ●

"I consider it best to use the far sides and edges of the tables as gauging points, as these will not have seen so much wear as the centre section of the tables"

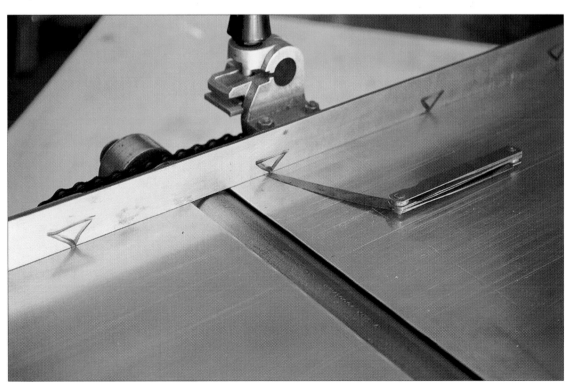

ABOVE: After any adjustment, the final check is completed with the DTI

RIGHT: Using a straight edge and feeler gauges, the in-feed table can be re-set off the out-feed table

Pinch up the fixings and re-check the levels.

The initial out-feed table setting is now complete and final checking and setting, using the DTI by gauging from the out-feed table face to the thicknesser table or the top face of the cutter-block, can be undertaken in a similar manner to that employed earlier when checking and setting the cutter-block from the thicknesser table.

Try to achieve the minimum run-out across the face of the table, and stick at it until the best possible compromise is achieved.

Step 7 Setting in-feed table to out-feed table

Having set both the cutter-block and out-feed table relative to the thicknesser table, you can proceed to set the in-feed table from the newly established out-feed table datum.

Ensure that the V-slide grooves in the table are clean and greased, and re-fit the table, making sure that the rectangular pressure pad washers are re-fitted in their original positions and directions.

Don't over-tighten the nuts holding the table to its sliders – equal pressure on each nut and pressure

pad is required so that the table slides smoothly with no stiff spots or rock over its full range of travel.

This in-feed table is now to be set relative to the out-feed table by use of a straight-edge and feelers. Place the straight-edge to take in the gauging points previously suggested – any adjustment necessary being accomplished in the same manner as that previously employed when setting the out-feed table.

Aim to achieve the best possible alignment. A final check with the DTI, gauging from the in-feed table to the cutter block, can be undertaken if you feel it is necessary.

Step 8 Re-commissioning

Carefully install and set a freshly-ground set of knives, at 40°. Next, lubricate all the moving parts and then re-fit and tension the drive-belts in their original direction of rotation – or treat the machine to a new set. Finally remove all dust from the motor and switch-gear and check the condition of the electrical wiring insulation for damage and cracks.

Last of all, check that all the tools have been removed, and turn the cutter-block over by hand to ensure a free rotation. Re-fit all the guards, re-connect the power supply and run the machine. Take test cuts in both the surfacing and thicknessing modes and make any small adjustments necessary to the out-feed table height and the thicknesser feed roller's spring tensions. ■

Bending the rules

Ray Smith looks at saw kerfing

PHOTOGRAPHY BY MANNY CEFAI

TO BE restricted to using only straight lines in designing furniture limits not only the aesthetic effect of a piece, but also its suitability for a specific function.

I wanted to make a small table to sit against the wall in our hallway and it got me thinking about the various ways that could be used to produce curved wooden components.

The table was to be about 914 by 330mm (3ft by13in) with a drawer in the centre, and a rounded top. I finally settled on a half elliptical top, four tapered legs joined with an elliptically curved skirt, with an elliptically curved drawer front between the two front legs. There was nothing much to it from a construction point of view, except for the elliptically curved skirts and drawer front.

Making curves

I discounted cutting from the solid because it would have meant starting with 50mm (2in) stock, which I didn't have, and it would have resulted in end-grain component in the visible skirts.

Likewise, steam-bending was ruled out because the curve on the elliptical skirts was fairly sharp and needed to be accurate.

Lamination would be quite wasteful on my limited supply of wood, and would take a great deal of effort and expense to make the formers.

I liked the idea of coopering as the grain could have run vertically which would have given an interesting cross-banding effect to the skirt, but vertical grain is not suitable on a drawer front.

Brick laid base and veneer was the traditional technique before power saws, planers and modern glues made lamination practicable. I could have used other wood for the bricks and would only need face veneer from my walnut. This technique was attractive, as the brick curve could be developed on a simple drawn template and could be hand-worked to an accurate fit before applying the facing veneers. This method seemed the most appropriate method as it involved no effort and cost to make the formers.

"I had read that kerfing was the technique traditionally used to form the bends in the sides of solid wood coffins"

Kerfing

However, I had read that kerfing was the technique traditionally used to form the bends in the sides of solid wood coffins – but if it was mentioned at all in books it was done so briefly, and dismissed as weakening the wood too much.

It occurred to me that if the bottoms of the kerfs, which don't close up under bending, are filled with veneer and glue, the loss of strength at the kerfed bend might well be sufficiently recovered. A few trials with some scrap off-cuts showed that kerfs re-enforced with veneer and Cascamite did indeed have plenty of strength and that, by altering the spacing of the kerfs, I could adjust the shape of the curve as I required – which was ideal for my elliptical application.

No formers are needed, so the curve can be achieved and reproduced accurately with no waste of wood. I felt that this was the method to go for, but I had to be careful that I did not split the thin laminate left after the kerfs are cut, and that the necessarily faceted surface could be shaped and smoothed to a clean curve.

ABOVE: An effective bending method that doesn't require expensive equipment

● **Following a career in the RAF as an Engineer Officer, RAY SMITH developed his interest in woodwork on a BTEC furniture course at Rycotewood College. Ray teaches woodwork and maths part-time and undertakes occasional commissions**

LEFT: The table that got Ray thinking about the construction methods of curves

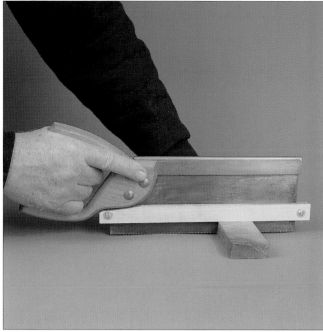

Method

I have done some analysis on exactly what happens when we bend wood by kerfing. The maths involved is not difficult, but rather than reproduce it I will describe my conclusions that are based on both theoretical and practical work.

1) To keep the strain in the wood, laminate within the limits the wood can sustain – and to prevent the facets between the kerfs being too pronounced to be smoothed out, the following limits should be applied:
a) Kerf width <5% wood thickness
b) Kerf depth >90% wood thickness
c) Radius of curve >150mm (6in)

2) Typically, this translates in 19 to 22mm (¾ to ⅞in) thick wood to leaving a 2mm (⁵⁄₆₄in) laminate at the base of the kerf, using a saw which produces a 1mm (½in) wide kerf, and not having kerfs closer than 9mm (⅜in).

3) The base of the kerf should be filled with a strip of standard 0.7mm thick veneer, of width about a third of the depth of the kerf, typically 6mm (¼in). This piece of veneer is used to drag Cascamite glue into the kerf and to ensure the cut surfaces are well covered.

4) The kerfed component is then bent until all the kerfs close up, and cramped across the ends until the glue is set. Then the facets can be smoothed off using a finely-set block or small smoothing plane, a cabinet scraper, and 120, 150, 230, and 320 cabinet abrasive papers. The amount of material to be removed to smooth out the facets will range from 0.25mm for a tight 150mm (6in) radius curve to <0.1mm for large radius curves, so you don't have to worry about cutting through your 2mm (⁵⁄₆₄in) laminate before you have smoothed the facets out.

5) It is more work, but good quality kerfing requires many kerfs cut with a thin saw to leave a thin laminate — using a wide saw and leaving a thick laminate (>2.5mm) certainly reduces the number of kerfs required for a given curve but involves a risk of splitting and leaving visible facets.

6) To produce accurate, consistent kerfs use a finely-set saw with strips of 6 by 20mm (¹⁵⁄₆₄ by ²⁵⁄₃₂in) squared wood, bolted across the blade to act as an accurate depth stop.
Remember, you are cutting 1mm (½in) wide kerfs to within 1.5 to 2.2mm (½ to ⁵⁄₆₄in) of wood thickness, so you need a consistent depth stop. I do not have one, but I would imagine a good quality hand mitre-saw would be ideal for this technique.
To calculate the spacing for your kerfs you need to find what angle each of your kerf's cut, with your particular saw set-up, produces. To do this, use an off-cut, the same thickness as your component wood and about 250mm (10in) long. Cut between 10 and 15 kerfs across the centre section of this piece at about 13mm (½in) intervals.
Veneer glue and cramp to close up the kerfs to form a curved piece with approximately 30mm (1³⁄₁₆in) straight ends – these ends will be turned from each other by between 25 to 50° depending on your kerfs.
When the test piece is dry, lay the piece on a paper and, using a ruler, produce the line of each straight end back over the curved portion. Use a protractor to measure the angle your kerfs have turned the ends of the piece through. Divide this angle by the number of the identical kerfs you cut and you have the measure of what each kerf is worth in practice – this should be between 2 and 4°.
Now, armed with this information and the full size rod drawing of your required curved component, you can space out your kerfs to achieve a kerf curved component accurately matched to your rod drawing – for example, supposing you want a part-circular component of 250mm (10in) radius to turn through 90° and the component curved length is 372mm (14⅝in). If your trial piece has shown each kerf is worth 3° then you will

"No formers are needed, so the curve can be achieved and reproduced accurately with no waste of wood"

MATHS FORMULA

Notation:
k = width of kerf
t = thickness of wood laminate at base of kerf
T = thickness of wood
r = Radius of curve measured to inside (concave) surface
R = Radius of curve measured to outside (convex) surface
D = Distance between centre lines of saw-cuts (kerfs)
a = Angle (in radian measure) of bend achieved by one kerf

The useful relationship equations are:
$a = k/(T-t)$ $r = D \times (T-t)/k$ $D = r \times k/(T-t)$ $R = r+T$
$R = D \times (T-t)/k+T$ $D = (R-T) \times k/(T-t)$ $D = r \times a$ $D = (R-T) \times a$

It is practical to have an 'a' = 3° or 0.0524 radians whence the depth of cut (T-t) must equal 19.1 x k so a 1mm kerf would require wood thickness T = 21 to 22mm and a 1.2mm kerf would require a wood thickness of 25mm. To use thinner woods a narrower kerf is required or 'a' the angle bent at each kerf would be too large. A 0.8mm kerf requires a wood thickness of 17 to 18mm.

It is best to find the achievable angle 'a' for a particular saw and depth of cut as described in the article, keeping 't' around 2mm 'T' can be settled on, or saws changed, to achieve a different 'k' so as to achieve an 'a' of 3°.

If you know the radius of curvature 'R' or 'r' you require the distance between kerfs D can be calculated from D = r x a or D = (R-T) x a

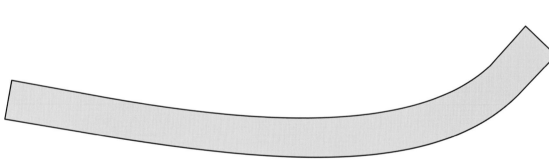

FIG 1

LEFT: By adjusting the spacing of the kerfs, the wood can be bent to conform to the curve required — here there are 15 kerfs, each worth 3°, with decreasing spacing, giving a tighter curve

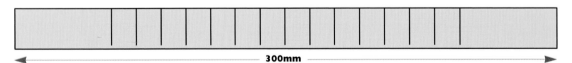

300mm

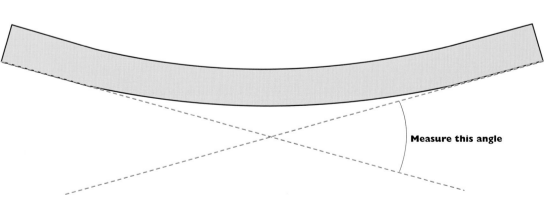

Measure this angle

FIG 2

LEFT: On a trial piece, cut 15 kerfs, glue-up and measure the angle — this angle, divided by 15 is the angle turned by each kerf

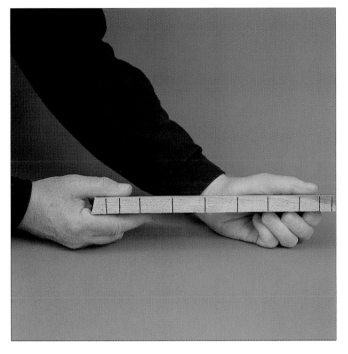

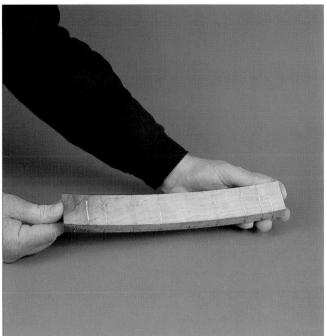

ABOVE LEFT: Kerfs cut – note the different spacing to allow for the flow of the curve

BELOW RIGHT: The kerfs are pushed together when glued-up

"The beauty of this method is that it enables any curved wooden component to be made accurately, without difficult and expensive-to-produce formers, and using simple hand tools"

BELOW: Cramped-up – note the veneer shims in the base of the kerfs to fill the area that won't close up – this ensures that there is no loss of strength

need to make 90/3=30 cuts evenly spaced at 372/31=12mm (¹⁵⁄₃₂in), that is, divide your wood into 31 by measuring at 12mm (¹⁵⁄₃₂in) intervals and saw your 30 kerfs.

After veneer gluing and bending, your component will turn in a smooth circular arc through 90° as required.

7) It is very easy to decide on kerf intervals for constant radius part-circular components, because the required number of kerfs for the required angle turned through will always be evenly spaced. For non-circular curves, as with my

elliptical table skirts, the spacing has to be less where the curve is tighter, and further apart as the curve flattens out. I used the mathematics of the ellipse to calculate the spacing, using a computer spreadsheet program – but it could have been done with sufficient accuracy using a full-size drawing and protractor.

The beauty of this method is that it enables any curved wooden component to be made accurately, without difficult and expensive-to-produce formers, and using simple hand tools. As I have used it to

date, on table skirts and drawer fronts, the strength is more than adequate and the closed kerfs on the concave surface and edges are not noticeable.

The method is probably not ideal for curved chair components where strength is paramount, but with the addition of veneer to the cut surfaces, I think that the strength could well be adequate, even for chair components.

It is certainly worth a trial – in my opinion, for one-offs, it is quicker, cheaper and easier than cutting from solid, steam bending, or laminating. ■

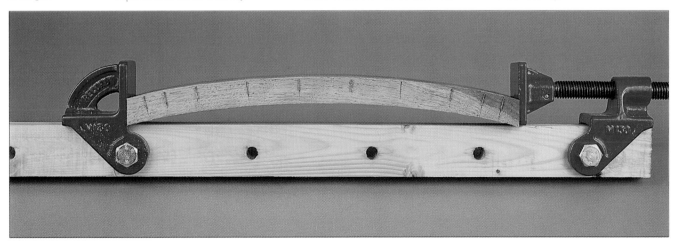

The X4 files

John Bennett looks back at the Marples X4 smoothing plane – a 1950s classic

Old friends

A GOOD TOOL is like a pair of well-fitting gloves or an old cardigan. However worn out or shabby they become, you can't quite part with them because they've become old friends.

Like most woodworkers, I have my favourite tools, and this story is about one of them.

Way back in my school days, when I was studying for my A-level in Woodwork at Taunton's School in Southampton, I had a teacher named Ted Luker. It was a school with a well established centre for craftsmanship and encouraged students to be innovative and work to high standards.

Ted came in one day with a brand new smoothing plane, a Marples X4, that he wanted me to use on an extended trial basis. He was keen to encourage students and used this as one way of doing so.

The plane

The plane was new on the market. It was traditional in many aspects and to a certain extent followed in the footsteps of others such as the Record and the Stanley, the undisputed quality makers of planes, although it looked different.

Up until then I had generally used smoothers with a 2⅜in blade, but this was only 2in. Comparing weights proved that the new plane was probably slightly heavier for its smaller blade width, but the overall length was much the same.

The blade was set at the usual angle of 45°. The depth of cut and lateral adjustment features were much the same as others. Depth adjustment was of the traditional Bailey-type, fine thread pattern screw, with the Y type of adjusting yoke.

The lateral adjustment lever was a strip of steel that was folded into a circle at the end, and two red plastic buttons were fixed into it for extra comfort – but that is where similarities ended.

The front knob was larger than average and was made of black lacquered wood, and was fixed in the traditional manner with a bolt threaded into the sole plate.

Surprises

The black stained wood handle projected about 1in beyond the heel and was built complete with the frog as an infill to the plane body – which was unusual for a new design in the mid 1950s.

The handle was secured to the base plate using three screws, two of which would normally hold the frog assembly in place. A surprise came when I found that the frog was not able to move back and forth as would be expected, because of this arrangement.

However, the biggest surprise was to discover the purpose of two screws on the inside, between the front knob and the mouth. They held an L-shaped piece of cast steel which was used to make the mouth adjustable.

That was something that no other plane in production had and, in those days when we were all using sapele and other rogue-grained timbers, this was to prove a tremendous asset, because the mouth width could be reduced allowing very fine setting of the cut.

ABOVE: **Fine adjustment of the mouth is allowed by the steel front mouth piece**

The sole was finished to a high standard, ground accurately and had no rough feel to it at all – something that cannot be said about most modern planes!

Blade assembly

Next came the inspection of the blade assembly – and again, there was something new. Although the lever cap iron was removed by the traditional cam mechanism, it was worked upside down, in that it was pivoted at the top and lifted from the bottom.

The lever cap iron was chrome plated but the lever itself was plated steel, finished with a black surface. The blade and cap iron were similar to others except that the blade was bevelled along its length on the grinding side.

The test

Now came the time to try it out. The blade was sharpened and the back of it was highly polished on progressively finer stones to make sure that it was flat, allowing accurate setting of the blade.

It was reassembled and made ready to plane a piece of wood. I tried it on a wide variety of species, with and against the grain, and on end-grain.

It was superb – and the more it was used the better it became!

Searching

However, I knew that I couldn't afford to buy one, especially as I had just bought a Stanley No.4, that was almost brand new, for 5/- (25p)!

The cost of the Marples X4 must have been about £2-15/- (£2.75) which was considerably more than a Stanley or Record.

For whatever reason, the plane was not a success and was removed from the catalogue quite quickly.

In the meantime I made a wooden smoother using a plan published by Charles Hayward in a paperback booklet on making tools. This I still use – but I really wanted one of those special planes, and I looked everywhere.

I answered adverts in the local paper, looked in junk shops, and when the specialist antique tool shops started up I kept enquiring – until, at a show in 1994, the Marples X4 smoothing plane was there!

I could not believe my eyes, I had almost given up hope of ever finding one. In fact so few people had heard of it that I was beginning to think that I had dreamed the story up – but there it was!

I paid a lot for it, but it was worth it, just to handle one again!

I took it home and went straight to the workshop. It was in beautiful condition and planed straight away. The blade is original but too soft, so I will replace it with a laminated blade and then it really will be this man's best friend! ■

ABOVE: **The lever cap iron**

BELOW: **The disassembled X4**

Lightening the load

Bob Wearing gives a lesson on chamfering in the Cotswold School manner

ABOVE: Chamfers help to define and soften the lines of a carcass

device to shed rainwater from horizontal surfaces, some to lighten the load pulled by horses and some purely for decoration, as on some wagons where chamfers were picked out in brilliantly contrasting hues.

The Cotswold Men took up the chamfer with enthusiasm, and it became one of the features which characterised their early pieces.

Chamfer appeal

The inside corners of carcasses and frames take chamfers, as do posts and legs. The appeal of the chamfer is the play of light between highly reflecting surfaces and deep shadows, *see photos.*

The very essence of chamfering is crispness, softened edges losing the sharp contrast between light and shade.

The skilled cabinetmaker of those days cut his chamfers by eye and a steady hand, but we lesser beings generally need some aid in the form of preliminary marking out.

If marking by pencil, a wipe of sanding sealer gives the pencil a bit of bite along the grain. I frequently use a fine ball-point pen if I am sure the surface will later be skimmed over.

The chamfer's width can easily be pencilled in, but a quarter circle at the corners presents a problem. If instead of the quarter circle this ends up as two arcs, they will screech at all who view them.

AT THE TURN of the century, the founders of the so-called Cotswold School, Gimson and the brothers Barnsley, left London to set up home and workshops in the Cotswolds.

Here they designed and made furniture entirely by hand, using native timbers. Rather than trying to pick up the threads of the great age of British furniture they decided to go right back to basics, making simple, honest pieces of immaculate workmanship.

The area was largely untouched by the industrial revolution, and the carpenters, barn builders, joiners, hurdle, ladder and gate-makers, wheelwrights and wainwrights all had the chamfer in common.

Some used the motif as a

> "The Cotswold Men took up the chamfer with enthusiasm, and it became one of the features which characterised their early pieces"

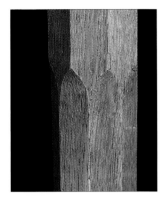

Marker

The answer is a simple chamfer gauge or marker. Over the years, several of these will accumulate. As students we carved these from ebony (*Diospyrus ebenum*) or rosewood (*Dalbergia sp*), and very elegant they looked.

These can be made less laboriously from two separate blocks.

Make a truly square block, about ³⁄₁₆ in thick (5mm), and gauge on two sides the width of chamfer required.

An elaborate geometrical construction can be used to find the centre of the required circle, but this manoeuvre is even more difficult on such a small scale. By far the easiest way to make the quarter circle is to find a suitable large washer, tin lid, plastic cap, coin, in fact anything round which fits; allow a shade for the thickness of the pencil.

Mark the arc, saw close and finish exactly – I use a disc sander. Make a smaller square and glue this in place, taking care that it does not slide from the gauged lines.

Before gluing, just nip off the inside corner. Remove all traces of excess glue and polish, or oil if you like.

To mark the chamfer, the joints must be cramped up, and the pencil must go precisely through that inside corner. Use the flat portion of the gauge to run the length of the workpiece. Never use a marking gauge for this.

Chamfers can be symmetrical, where the width is the same on both marked surfaces, or asymmetrical – where one is wider than the other – requiring two chamfer gauges.

ABOVE: Chamfer gauges

Drawknives

The chief chamfering tool is the drawknife. The wheelwright's tool, as big as a bicycle handlebar, is not designed for this purpose. Just the job, however, is the 'gent's drawknife' with a blade of, say, 6in.

In Victorian times there were a number of 'gent's' tools, of which the only survivors are the drawknife and the 'gent's backsaw'. These were tools of high quality, smaller and lighter than the tradesman's and made for middle and upper class gentlemen amateurs.

Sharpness is, of course, essential, and a rather stubby bevel works better than a very thin one. I tend to guide the tool with one hand, the other – depending on how the workpiece is held – either resting on the benchtop or tucked into the waist.

Naturally, the corner is worked first, finishing with a very fine continuous full-width cut. Most of the waste on the parallel

section is removed by drawknife, generally used bevel down but bevel up if the grain is sympathetic. A difficult spot can arise if the curve joins rising grain; then the direction must be changed and the cut kept fine.

Whatever the 'old men' did, today most woodworkers finish the straight portion with a flat-faced iron spokeshave; on a very long chamfer a small block plane may be used.

The critical point is where the curve blends into the parallel. Use the finger rather than the eye to detect any bump, which will certainly show up when polished.

Small chamfers can be started with a stubby chisel, but this really is a last resort.

One book recommends a half-round file – sheer heresy; according to precedent this should be burnt!

If no-one is looking, the merest touch of a scraper is sometimes applied. Held literally flat, and pushed, this can take out a

LEFT: Components cramped together and chamfers marked

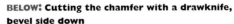
BELOW: Cutting the chamfer with a drawknife, bevel side down

● BOB WEARING has spent a lifetime teaching woodwork and furniture design. A respected author on the subjects, his titles include The Essential Woodworker, The Resourceful Woodworker and Hand Tools for Woodworkers, all published by Batsford. He also contributes to F&C's new sister publication The Router.

ABOVE LEFT: Half-twist chamfer on octagonal table leg

ABOVE MIDDLE: Double-twist chamfer on walnut pedestal leg

ABOVE RIGHT: Strong asymmetrical chamfers on table base

minute blemish without loss of straightness or flatness.

Chamfers should never be sanded as they will lose that vital crispness. Oil or wax finishes are suitable, but varnish or lacquer will clog up and lose the crispness, except perhaps on very large work.

Other chamfers

Two other forms of chamfer are the common stopped chamfer – a joiner's motif often found on garden gates – for which a simply made chiselling aid is employed, and the spokeshave chamfer, often used by those lacking either courage or a drawknife – or both.

This tool should not be denigrated as in some situations it can be most effective. It was often used in school when real woodwork was taught.

Is it cheating to rout? Some think so while others feel the router to be a legitimate time-saving tool since chamfering by hand is not quick.

If a router is used, its 45° cutter must be big enough to span the finished width as the job cannot be done in two bites.

In this case, the parallel portion is worked first, finishing to size. The drawknife then cuts the curved ends and blends into the routing.

To machine asymmetrical chamfers I use an overhead routing system and a tilting table; no doubt there are other ways. Wide, flat, error-revealing chamfers need extreme care and are the most difficult to do perfectly.

Chamfers are most effective on the coarser-grained British woods – oak (*Quercus robur*), elm (*Ulmus procera*), ash (*Fraxinus excelsior*), chestnut (*Castanea sativa*) and walnut (*Juglans regia*). They are not so effective on sycamore (*Acer pseudoplatanus*) and certainly not on the imported mahoganies (*Swietenia macrophylla*) and their like, for which fine mouldings are more suited.

Like all decoration, chamfering should be planned in detail beforehand, not applied as an afterthought. ■

TOP: Joiner's chamfer and template

ABOVE: Cutting stops with the template

BELOW: Finished chamfers

ABOVE LEFT: Cutting the flat with a drawknife, bevel side up

LEFT: Tidying up with the spokeshave

Predicting the spring

Bill Clayden offers a calculated approach to the problem of spring-back of laminations

ABOVE: **Grating chair with laminated components in the seat and back**

F URNITURE-MAKERS will know only too well that spring-back occurs when a curved laminate is removed from its former; this can make designing pieces which incorporate such components a hit-and-miss affair.

Received wisdom states that more plies means less spring-back, but doesn't tell us how much less. The only advice I could find was to use trial and error, which I consider to be wasteful of time and material, particularly for one-offs.

I became interested in this problem recently when I made a pair of chairs from reclaimed teak, *see panel.*

Since the laminations are not all supported by a rigid frame – in particular the three rails in the back of the chair, laminated from four, five and six plies respectively – I needed to know how much the laminates would deviate from the curve of the former when the clamps were released.

Analysing problem

My scientific and engineering background led me to look into the problem analytically. I discovered that for many situations a delightfully simple solution follows from the application of simple beam-bending theory – taught at first year engineering degree level and found in virtually all textbooks dealing with stress analysis.

The problem is illustrated in the diagram, *see fig 1.*

A number of laminations, 'n', are glued and clamped to a curved former which is shaped to give the laminations a radius of 'R'. When the clamps are removed the laminations spring away from the former, and the radius increases by 'r'.

The problem is to determine 'r' in terms of all the relevant parameters such as the radius of the former, the number of laminations, and the properties and thickness of the individual laminations.

Formula

If it is assumed that:-
(a) all the laminations are made from the same timber and are machined to the same section,
(b) the thickness of the glue line is negligible compared with the thickness of the laminations,
(c) there is no shearing movement between laminations along the glue line, and
(d) the thickness of the lamination is small compared with the radius of the former, then the solution is given by the following simple formula:
$r = R(n^2 - 1)$.

Thus the spring-back depends only on the number of laminations and not on the properties or thickness of the wood or the geometry of the curved former.

The formula illustrates the well known fact that more laminations mean less spring-back. It also enables the spring-back to be readily quantified so that the radius of the former can be adjusted accordingly.

Since this book is devoted to cabinetmaking and not stress analysis, the details of the derivation of the formula are omitted. However it has recently been independently verified and was apparently first derived in 1957, *see page 69 for details.*

Validity

In theory the analysis could be extended to include laminates containing woods of different sizes and properties, also to allow for a particular glue line

LEFT: **Photo 1 Spring-back from a curved former**

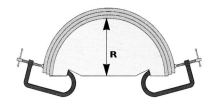

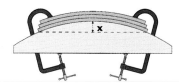

Laminations clamped to former radius 'R'

'n' laminations clamped to former

"When I derived the formula for spring-back I was concerned with laminating components which had a relatively large radius"

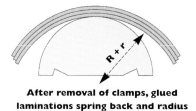

After removal of clamps, glued laminations spring back and radius increases by 'r'

Fig 1 Springback from a curved former

After removal of clamps, glued laminations spring back by a distance of 'y'

Fig 2 Springback from a large radius former

thickness and some shear movement; however this solution would be so complex and specific to the precise component that I doubt if the exercise would be worthwhile.

The above assumptions should hold true for most practical, furniture-making purposes.

In most situations assumption (a) will be valid since curved components will probably be laminated from plies of similar thickness and type of timber.

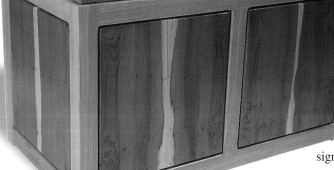

The formula will still hold if the laminations are identical in shape, although each individual lamination may have a varying thickness throughout its length.

It is possible that the two outer plies of a laminate will be made from more valuable timber than the inner plies, although the thicknesses of the inner and outer plies may be different. In this case the formula will not be strictly valid, but will give a better starting point than just guessing.

The glue line's thickness, assumption (b), may be easily measured before and after gluing and clamping. A few measurements made with a vernier show it is only a few hundredths of a millimetre – negligible for most practical purposes.

Shear movement along the glue line, assumption (c), is negligible provided a glue is used which does not 'creep' significantly, such as Cascamite or Aerolite, and not PVA.

Assumption (d), that the thickness of the lamination is small compared with the radius of the former, must necessarily hold because timber cannot be bent cold round a radius which is much less than about 50 times its thickness without significant breakage.

Simpler formula

When I derived the above formula I was concerned with laminating components which

had a relatively large radius, i.e. those for the seats and backs of chairs, and here the curve is specified by the deflection from a straight line rather than the radius.

In this case the formula may be approximated to give an even simpler formula, *see fig 2*. A number of laminations, 'n', are glued and clamped to a curved former which is shaped to give the laminations a deflection of 'x'. When the clamps are removed the laminations spring away from the former by an amount 'y'. Using the same assumptions as before, the spring back is given by: $y = x/n^2$.

To illustrate, for two laminations the spring-back is 1/4 of the initial deflection, 1/9 for three laminations, 1/16 for four laminations, and so on.

Put another way, if a bent component of 10mm (3/8in) final thickness were laminated from two laminations 5mm (13/64in) thick, the spring-back would be $1/2^2 = 1/4$, which is quite significant.

If the same component were laminated from 10 laminations 1mm (3/64in) thick, the spring-back would be $1/10^2 = 1/100$ which, for virtually all practical woodworking purposes, may be ignored.

For the slack curves illustrated above I made the former out of second-hand 3 by 2in and either drew the shape by eye, fairing the curve with a spline and weights, or used a method employed by loftsmen on the mould loft floor in a shipyard to draw curved deck beams for which the radius is much bigger than the length of the loft.

LEFT: Rocking chair with laminated components

"The analysis could be extended to include laminates containing woods of different sizes and properties"

For those interested in pre-CAD geometric construction for curves of large radius, several methods are given in *A text book of laying off*, by Attwood and Cooper, a title that may bring a wry smile to some readers.

Chair construction

My chair components were made from two to six plies; the few measurements taken in my workshop with a standard steel rule demonstrate how well the formula works.

Based on the discussion above and some limited measurements, I concluded that for practical purposes the assumptions are valid.

Stacks of laminations are shown glued up and clamped to a former, *see photo 2*, and then released after the glue has set. The laminations spring away from the former by a small amount, which is consistent with the prediction.

I have used the formula when constructing two other pieces of furniture, *see photos*, and obtained further evidence that the formula works in practice.

Practical tests

The ash rocking chair components are laminated from a number of plies as follows: transverse battens of the seat – two; runners – three; longitudinal bearers of the seat – four; legs – five, the number of laminations being determined by the maximum radius that a lamination may be bent when cold without breaking.

This data is given in the textbooks, but a quick rule of thumb for pliable woods such as ash is that a radius of 50 times

the ply's thickness will be on the safe side.

The battens for the curved top of the chest shown are laminated from a 6mm, $^1/_4$ in ash outer ply and a 6mm cedar of Lebanon inner ply. Despite the different timbers, the formula still works sufficiently well for the laminated battens to lie nicely on the relatively light frame of the lid without requiring any significant cramping pressure.

So for practical purposes the formula may probably be applied to laminations composed of differing woods. At least it would be better than making no allowance or just guessing. ■

AUTHOR'S ACKNOWLEDGEMENT

As a result of a chance meeting with Peter Guyett, a professional engineer, we discussed the spring-back problem. Peter independently verified my analysis, made helpful suggestions and encouraged me to write this article. I would like to express my sincere thanks to him. Since the publication of this article in *Furniture & Cabinetmaking* magazine I have discovered that essentially the same results were given by Stevens and Turner in *Spring-back of laminated bends*, WOOD, February 1957. These results were not widely disseminated amongst craft woodworkers.

ECONOMY AND STYLE

THE TEAK from which the chairs were made came from windows replaced at a local transmitting station by modern aluminium double-glazed units. Fortunately a friend of mine who works at the station and, like me, served an apprenticeship as a shipwright in a naval dockyard, appreciated the value of the teak, rescuing the frames from the inevitable bonfire.

I wanted to use the reclaimed material economically and to good effect.

Because the frames had numerous joints,

fastenings and drain holes, conversion of the timber into useful sizes dictated a design including some fairly large components, such as chair legs and rails, and numerous small components such as the curved members of the seat and back – laminated from stock about 5mm, $^{13}/_{64}$ in thick.

Having always admired the decorative effect achieved by using teak gratings as hard-wearing walkways and cockpit floors on high class ships and yachts, I decided to incorporate this detail.

To distinguish my

ABOVE: Economical use of reclaimed teak

work from mass-produced teak or iroko garden furniture the seat and back of the chair have conical surfaces. This not only enhances the appearance, but provides an interesting technical challenge.

Hand veneering

F&C Editor **Paul Richardson** says that veneering the traditional way is cheap, fast and effective — so why aren't we all doing it?

A case for veneering

THERE WAS A time when cabinetmaking, as a trade, didn't exist in Britain. Furnituremaking techniques were no different to those used in other areas of woodworking — primary construction, joinery and so on — and so the construction of furniture was just another function of turners, joiners, carvers and upholsterers.

With the restoration of the monarchy in the mid-seventeenth century, however, came a new age of extravagance in the arts and crafts as the sombre Puritan era gave way to the self-indulgence that was to last nearly 200 years, until the Victorians rediscovered earnestness.

Greater skill

From the point of view of the furnituremaker, the most important aspect of this period is the introduction of veneering. This was a skill not required of turners, joiners or carvers, and so created a new class of craftsman: "The cabinet-maker, whose craft was established with the introduction of veneering" as "Veneering demands greater skill,

and cabinet-making, as distinct from joiners' work, is practised by specially skilled craftsmen" (*John Gloag's Dictionary of Furniture*, revised by Dr Clive Edwards, ISBN 0-04-440774-2).

The extraordinary work created in the 'golden age of furniture' that was to follow in the eighteenth century would not have been possible without veneering, or cabinetmakers to do it.

As we owe the very existence of the craft to hand veneering, it's surprising that more of us don't do it. Modern work lends itself to the use of veneers, and from an environmental point of view veneering over a groundwork of, say, MDF makes a lot of sense.

The real benefit of veneering is its ability to create decorative effects which are impossible using solid timbers, whether it is because the species chosen is unstable in the solid, for example burrs and highly figured crotches with a lot of short grain, or because the construction can't be achieved in solid without laminating or joining, for example a tightly curved component.

Techniques

A hot-press is an efficient device for covering a large square footage, but is too large and expensive for the cabinetmaker so is operated by a sub-contractor, with a resultant loss of control and time spent delivering, waiting and collecting.

Cold-presses are more affordable, but again they are unwieldy beasts and take up a lot of space if they are large enough to be useful.

Vacuum-bag presses are useful, but again are relatively expensive — especially if large enough to press a 10ft long table top.

Caul veneering — whereby the veneer is clamped to the groundwork and the pressure is spread by a caul, similar to that used for laminating — is cheap but requires a lot of preparation.

Compare these to hand veneering with Scotch glue. This is an immediate process with no waiting — either for sub-contractors or while every clamp in the workshop is holding a caul in place.

Most cabinetmakers already have much of the equipment needed, but if not it is cheap and takes up barely any space, regardless of the size of the work.

Best of all, laying veneer by hand is controllable and reversible, so adjustments can be made during the process — not possible with any of the other methods. Unlike most hand processes, veneering is very quick, outpacing even a hot-press for some work. The maker can, for example, veneer all six faces of a box in a single sitting. Curves present no special problems, nor do they require complicated shaped cauls to be made for every new job.

No swearing

But surely, as stated above, "Veneering demands greater skill…"? Not in my experience — I find hanging wallpaper much more challenging!

I have seen people get into a real mess with Scotch glue and veneer, though, and more workshop swearing has been provoked by this than by any other process — except maybe laminating — which is saying something. Looking at most published descriptions of the process this is not surprising, as one or two crucial stages always seem to be left out — more of these later.

I was fortunate to be taught hand veneering in a commercial cabinet shop, where a few men produced dozens of pieces of furniture "in the Georgian manner" every month, so their approach was of the no-nonsense variety, and well-proven.

Although some one-offs were produced there, most of the work involved small batches — maybe four or six pieces at a time — which requires a disciplined approach without needless messing around.

This suits hand veneering. The mistake most people make is to proceed carefully and thoughtfully, taking stock of progress before moving on to the next stage — just as one should with cabinet work.

In fact successful veneering must be carried out at a fair pace; stopping to think or check progress is asking

for trouble. The reversible nature of Scotch glue makes it unnecessary anyway, as if something hasn't quite worked it is easy enough to sort it out later.

Heat and moisture

The two things that matter most when using Scotch glue are heat and moisture; too little or too much of either will cause problems. If the glue is at the correct temperature when it comes out of the gluepot then it will be too cold after a minute or so — spend that minute thinking about what to do next and it's too late.

A heated iron can be used to warm up the glue if this happens — this will be discussed later — but adding dry heat in this way removes moisture, and too little of this is as bad as too little heat.

Rather than having to deal with the problem of rapidly chilling glue, which becomes a sticky jelly rather than the desired liquid, simply get the veneer down before it happens. Then as the glue chills it will hold the veneer in place while it sets, and everything works as it should.

Planning

This is all very well, but doesn't leave any time for thinking; and cabinetmakers like to plan their next move with the care and precision of a cat with a mouse.

The solution is to do all the thinking before picking up the glue brush; plan exactly what needs to be done from start to finish. Make sure that everything that you will need is within easy reach — you won't have time to go looking for that knife halfway through. Prepare the veneer and the groundwork properly, see that the glue is at the right temperature and consistency, clear your working area and take the phone off the hook.

● **In the following article Paul Richardson veneers a panel to illustrate the technique**

Tools and equipment

Hot water

Veneering, like childbirth, calls for copious amounts of hot water on demand. If your workshop has the luxury of running hot water then all you have to do is turn the thermostat up, but in the more likely event that it doesn't a water heater is essential.

If mains water is available then an electric water heater can be plumbed in, and will top itself up as water is drawn. Second-hand examples are easy to find — if you have any trouble ask your local electrician — but choose the largest you can fit in. Ten litres is the smallest worth considering, but 25 or even 50 litres would be better.

If, like me, mains water in your workshop is a distant dream, then a portable unit is the only option. I'm sure that they can be bought new, but mine cost me the princely sum of £5 at a school fete.

To hold the water a bucket is needed — plastic, and with a handle — and to apply it a piece of worn towelling about 300mm, 12in square. Bar towels are perfect, but ask first!

Glue, pots and brushes

Scotch glue must be kept at a suitable temperature but without direct heat, which means a proper gluepot — the biggest investment. For very occasional use a double-skinned pot such as that made by Liberon (about £38) on a hotplate is adequate, but these need some looking after as they have water between the two skins and mustn't boil dry.

For any serious use a water-free, thermostatically-controlled electric gluepot is a must, but they are expensive. The only model I could find in the UK was the Barlow Whitney 4pt device, *pictured*, which would cost about £230 to replace, although they make a 2pt version which sells for less than £200. The Garret Wade catalogue shows a

ABOVE: Clockwise: ancient Morphy-Richards iron, veneer hammer and Warrington pattern hammer.

smaller example in both 115V and 230V forms, a real bargain at $95.

Glue is brushed on; I eschew the traditional wire-bound glue brush in favour of a masonry-paint brush.

Not a tool, but perhaps equipment, is Scotch glue. These days most often sold in pearl form, it is diluted with water and heated for use.

Laying down

To press down the veneer a veneer 'hammer' is used. I discovered recently that these can be bought for about £12, but they are quick and easy to make, *see panel.* A real, Warrington pattern, hammer is useful for laying crossbanding.

A heated iron will be needed. Older, heavy irons are best so once again I rummage around for second-hand examples, but if stealing the family iron bear in mind that steam irons have holes in their soles and are, therefore, useless.

"Veneering, like childbirth, calls for copious amounts of hot water on demand"

RIGHT: Clockwise from front: pearl Scotch glue, electric glue pot and Liberon double-skinned pot.

ABOVE: Clockwise – veneer saw, old chisels, Stanley knives, steel rule, old square, cutting gauge and knife made from machine hacksaw blade.

Cutting

As will be seen later, when hand veneering most of the trimming and cutting of joins is carried out while the veneer is wet with glue, so a knife is used. A curved veneer saw might be useful for initial preparation, but I've never used mine for veneer at all.

The good old Stanley knife is as good a tool as any, and certainly the blades of these tools come in handy for mitring crossbanding. I use these and a knife made from a used machine-hacksaw blade.

A luxury item for preparing crossbanding is a paper-guillotine. These are in no way essential, but if you see one second-hand pick it up.

A cutting gauge is essential, and an old square is handy. Scotch glue contains salt and there is a lot of water about when veneering, so keep a couple of old chisels (where do you buy old chisels?), 25mm, 1in and 10mm, $^3/_8$in, say, for this purpose, together with an old steel rule. ■

ABOVE: Paper guillotine; useful for cutting crossbanding but not essential.

NOT A HAMMER AT ALL

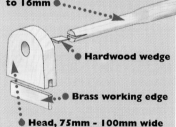

**Handle
200mm long
21mm diameter, tapering to 16mm**

● **Hardwood wedge**

● **Brass working edge**

● **Head, 75mm – 100mm wide**

The veneer hammer is easily made from offcuts. The handle is about 200mm, 8in long and wedge-tenoned into the head, which should be around 75mm, 3in wide. Set into the lower edge of the head is a piece of brass with its outer edge gently rounded. A 75mm, 3in brass butt hinge with its knuckle filed flush and polished may be used.

Hand veneering

In part two,
F&C Editor
Paul Richardson
explains the basics of
making it stick

PHOTOGRAPHY BY ANTHONY BAILEY

IN PART ONE I put the case for hand veneering, and claimed that there was no reason for it to present a problem to anyone with a minimum of equipment provided that each step is followed.

In this article I will discuss the steps involved in applying a plain veneer, Brazilian mahogany (*Swietenia macrophylla*) in this case, to a groundwork. No crossbanding or other sophistications as these will be dealt with later, for now just the basic 'wallpaper' technique of hammer veneering on which more complex work is built.

First steps

First prepare the glue and the veneer, *see panels*.

Soaking veneer is one of the steps least often mentioned in any written explanation of the process, but is crucial to success. If dry veneer comes into contact with hot, wet glue then it will expand, twist and buckle in just the same way as solid woods react to heat and moisture.

Soaking the veneer in advance means that this movement takes place before it is laid – this is better than trying to lay a veneer while it is changing shape!

The following steps should each be undertaken as quickly as possible, and in rapid succession.

Make sure that the groundwork is free of dust and grease, and brush a little more than half of it with glue. Quickly position the first piece of veneer onto the glued surface, smoothing it down with the hand.

The next step is almost never mentioned in descriptions of hand veneering, and that is to brush glue onto the top of the veneer.

Why is this done? Like soaking, it encourages the veneer to behave itself in accordance with the first principle of stability: never do

LEFT: Plain-veneered sideboard by the author in Brazilian rosewood with boxwood line inlay – complex techniques are not necessary for an effective result.

anything to just one face of a piece of wood. A well-known example: if just one face of a board is veneered then unequal stresses will cause it to warp, so a balancing veneer is applied to the other face (not always – *see below*).

When the underside of veneer is placed onto hot, wet glue it will buckle unless glue is applied to the top face. Additionally, veneer saturated with glue in this way will be less prone to splintering when dry.

Iron and hammer

Having done this, apply a heated iron if necessary.

On a warm day, and with an area of veneer smaller than a square metre, an iron probably won't be needed. If used it should be swept quickly over the whole surface to heat the glue, not attempting to press down the veneer. Be careful not to dry out the veneer or, once again, it will buckle; too much dry heat will

> "On no account stop moving the iron, or it will stick with disastrous consequences"

also evaporate the water in the glue, making it too thick to be expelled in the next stage.

On no account stop moving the iron, or it will stick with disastrous consequences.

Next take the veneer hammer and press down the veneer with considerable force, trying to squeeze out all of the glue. Of course this isn't possible, but for the veneer to stick properly a wood-to-wood join must be achieved.

Until the glue sets, the veneer will be held in place by a combination of Scotch's initial tackiness, and the partial vacuum created by expelling all air and glue.

Start in the middle by making

GLUE PREPARATION

ABOVE: Pearl glue in soak.

ABOVE: Judging the correct consistency.

SCOTCH GLUE is most often sold in pearl form, which is quick and easy to prepare.

Put a quantity of pearl in a non-metallic container and add cold water to more than cover the glue.

When the water has been absorbed about an hour later, put most of the now rubbery pearls into the gluepot to heat.

Add water a little at a time once the glue has liquefied, until it runs from the brush in a steady stream, *see picture*. If it hangs from the brush it is too thick, if it breaks up into droplets it is too thin and more soaked pearl must be added.

Use fresh glue every time: once Scotch has hardened it loses some of its workability.

ABOVE: Brushing glue onto the groundwork.

ABOVE: Warm the glue with an iron – keep it moving.

> "Handling a cloth in very hot water is a little painful, but becomes less so with practice"

strokes the full length of the veneer, holding the hammer at an angle, *see picture*, so that the glue squeezes out at the side nearest the edge of the veneer, in its 'wake'. Overlapping the strokes, continue until the edge is reached and the surplus glue emerges. Return to the middle and repeat the process, this time holding the hammer at the opposite angle and working out to the other side.

Quickly hammer round all four edges, all the while angling the hammer towards the outside of the veneer.

If there is much glue visible on the surface, soak a cloth in water that is as hot as you can stand, and wring it out until it is almost dry. Wipe the veneer, *as described below*.

Overlapping join

The second piece of veneer is laid in the same way as the first, but overlapping it by half an inch or so. Lay a wooden straight edge along the

mid-point of the overlap and knife through both thicknesses.

Do this with two or three strokes; the first should be quite gentle but held firmly against the straight edge to avoid the knife following the grain, the second or third cut should be through to the groundwork.

Now remove the waste from the top layer, then carefully peel up the top veneer and pull out the waste from that below. If it has stuck firm, brush a line of hot glue along it; this will soften the glue, holding the veneer enough for it to be gently peeled away.

Press down the join with the hand, brush a line of hot glue over it and hammer down – this time angling the hammer towards the join, through which the surplus glue should emerge.

Wring out the cloth and wipe the entire surface quickly and firmly, being careful not to snag any of the veneer's edges.

It is very important that the cloth is hot and merely moist, not wet, as adding more water at this stage is a bad idea. The aim is just to melt the unwanted glue, picking it up on the cloth as it is rubbed over the surface. Rub firmly, and do not go over the veneer more than once.

Handling a cloth in very hot water is a little painful, but becomes less so with practice. Rubber gloves might help, but I find that they make me clumsy – perhaps just one on the non-dominant hand might be a good idea.

Blisters

While the veneer is still damp catch the light on the surface, looking for the gentle bump that indicates a blister. If any are found, press them with a dry hammer that has been warmed in hot water; if this doesn't work then leave a weight on the spot, preventing it from sticking with a scrap of paper placed in between.

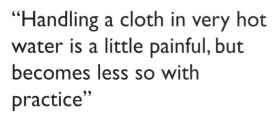

ABOVE: **Smoothing the veneer onto the glued groundwork.**

ABOVE: **Applying glue to the top of the veneer.**

ABOVE: **Hammering down straight after the iron.**

ABOVE: **Note the angle of the hammer – working towards the outer edge.**

VENEER PREPARATION

WHEN HAND
veneering, most cutting, joining and matching is carried out as the veneer is being laid, so the only preparation needed is to soak it.

Select the leaves that you intend to use and cut them well over-size. Sponge both sides of the veneer with a well wrung-out cloth soaked in near-boiling water, then put it in a stack between two pieces of chipboard or MDF. Place a weight on the top board and leave it for a while.

How long veneer needs to be left under pressure varies with its species,

ABOVE: **Sponging veneer with hot water.**

type of cut and its age – a fresh mahogany will need only 15 minutes or so, an old, buckled rosewood (*Dalbergia sp*) might need three or four hours. Some difficult burrs are best left overnight.

Leave each leaf between the boards until the moment it is used.

ABOVE: **Cleaning off surplus glue.**

ABOVE: Cutting through the overlapped join.

ABOVE: Peeling out the surplus.

ABOVE: Brush the join with glue and hammer down.

> "Many blisters that are apparent while wet have vanished when the veneer and groundwork have dried – but those that remain have to be found by stealth"

RIGHT: Clean off with a hot damp cloth, then leave to dry.

In fact many blisters that are apparent while wet have vanished when the veneer and groundwork have dried – but those that remain have to be found by stealth.

Brush your fingers across the dry surface, listening for a change of sound – a dry whisper. If this is heard, lightly tap the area where it occurred. You are now listening for a click, rather than the dull noise heard when your fingers tap sound veneer, indicating a gap between veneer and groundwork.

Ninety-nine per cent of such dry blisters can be pressed down with a heated iron – use just the edge and only on the area of the blister – a quick stroke should do the trick. More stubborn examples require strategies that will be covered another time.

Staying flat

According to the principle quoted above, the obverse of the panel should now be veneered to balance the stresses. I have never fully accepted this as many pieces of antique furniture have components which are veneered on only one side, yet remain flat.

One answer is that these parts – table tops, carcass sides, door panels, drawer fronts – are restrained by the furniture's construction.

However, some time ago I was shown a simple technique. If the freshly veneered component is laid face-down on newspaper until fully dry, it stays flat. I have no idea why this works, but work it does. ▪

Pressing issues

Veneering: **Andrew Skelton** suggests Paul Richardson steps into the twentieth century – leaving his glue pot behind

I WAS INTRIGUED to read that the Editor, Paul Richardson, finds veneering with Scotch glue "easier than hanging wallpaper", *see pages 70–76*. While I am delighted that he has revealed the mysteries, I'm in no hurry to adopt the technique.

I don't like hanging wallpaper and I enjoy the wet, sticky business of hand-veneering even less. I like my veneers neatly taped and stuck down with a good modern glue under plenty of pressure – all hit, no miss and no mess.

For the price of Paul's minimal equipment list – glue pot at anything up to £230, second-hand water heater at £5 (more like £205 for the not so lucky) – you could be well on the way to buying a vacuum press. With a vacuum press flat veneering is just the beginning – simple and compound curves can be laminated and the imagination can run riot.

Vacuum press

For those who haven't seen this wonderful piece of appropriate technology it consists quite simply of a pump which pulls the air from a thick plastic bag in which the work is placed.

Drawing the air from the bag allows atmospheric pressure, 14.7lbs per sq. inch, to bear in all directions on the work.

In practice the pump may pull only 90 per cent of a full vacuum, but even so the pressure is considerable and very effective. Not only does the

> "I like my veneers neatly taped and stuck down with a good modern glue under plenty of pressure – all hit, no miss and no mess"

RIGHT: Cabinet in veneered and solid cherry – note the crossbanded carcass edges

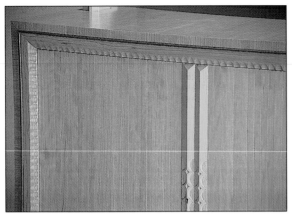

> "When a supplier receives the confession that bits of wood are going to be put in a plastic bag he will come out with the standard reply: We'll get back to you"

RIGHT & BELOW: The veneered and laminated birch ply back of this chair was formed in the vacuum press

vacuum apply pressure, it also draws glue into the pores of the wood.

The press is ideal for flat veneering, but it really excels when laminating curves. The small workshop can attempt complex curves and large curved panels as it is only necessary to build the male mould rather than the perfectly matched male and female moulds demanded by conventional presses.

I have watched glass fibre motorbike parts being made in a vacuum bag with incredible results.

Obsolete

Not only does the vacuum press replace hand-veneering, it makes many of those complex and multi-cramped jigs obsolete, in many instances out-performing the conventional, large and expensive screw press.

Few small workshops can afford to dedicate a large area to a press, but the vacuum press consists simply of a platen – probably 2400 by 1200mm (96 by 48in) melamine faced chipboard – which can lean against the wall, a bag that will roll up and a small pump.

Veneers can be lined up, or laminates aligned on moulds; the transparency of the bags enables observation of the application of pressure. Problems can be spotted in time for a retry – assuming the glue will permit this.

Getting started

Two main types of vacuum pump are available – the venturi which runs off a compressor, and the rotary vane which has its own integral motor. Sourcing pumps and the appropriate fittings can prove a fraught business.

Vacuum pumps have many applications in industry; outlets which deal with compressed air may also supply vacuum pumps, gauges and fittings.

A supplier will inevitably want to know what the equipment is needed for; when he receives the confession that bits of wood are going to be put in a plastic bag he will come out with the standard reply: "We'll get back to you."

Of course, he'll file you under I for idiot and hope you'll go away, but don't despair.

Money can be saved by buying the bits and pieces separately, but I recommend going for the purpose-made kit which has become available since I assembled my press.

The bags can be real problem; although I had mine strongly welded by a tarpaulin manufacturer, the bulk of the weld made achieving a good seal difficult. The acquisition of an Air Press bag with an easy close mechanism brought with it the realisation of how simple this could be and how efficiently the press could work.

Pressure switch

A good bag and fittings that don't leak will hold a vacuum for some time – even hours – and many pumps are designed for continuous running.

LEFT: The problem cornice topping these structures meant a return to Scotch glue

If making your own system, a pressure release valve will be needed to protect the pump, and a one-way valve to not only protect work, but maintain the vacuum when the pump is turned off.

Even if pumping continuously a one-way valve is essential – an interruption to my power supply once stopped the pump, the rush of escaping air set it rotating the wrong way and when the power came back on a couple of seconds later the pump was filling the bag; luckily the glue had already cured, but I bought a one-way valve all the same.

Limitations

While the vacuum press is versatile and relatively cheap, it has its drawbacks.

In a subsequent article I will be looking at some of the processes of veneering and laminating, but for now I shall use examples of my work to illustrate employment of the vacuum bag.

Veneering should not be thought of as an inexpensive alternative to using solid wood. It has, in some quarters, a reputation of cheapness but, as with any other surface treatment in the small, non-specialised workshop – painting, gilding, covering with leather – the process is far from cheap.

Veneering allows effects that are impossible to achieve in solid timber, the use of otherwise unusable cuts and, of course, represents an important economy in the amount of prime timber used.

Conflicting dogmas

Using veneering simply to replace solid timber is often the more expensive option.

Besides, perhaps I am too caught up in the dogmas of both the Arts and Crafts Movement – structural honesty – and the Modern Movement – form and function – but I feel that veneering has its own language, seen in the best of old work using burr, crotch and marquetry.

By contrast, the work that gives veneering a bad reputation uses veneer to imitate solid wood. In my cherry cupboard, the veneers are cross-grain and 'fold' round the edges, so could not be solid timber. The solid cherry, on the other hand, is carved to prove its substance.

Bitten by bug

Those introduced to the technique will soon find it is a whole lot more than a bit of MDF and a few veneers; methods will have to be found to solve the new constructional problems that this new world presents.

Many makers use solid timber and bandsawn veneers to allow them to construct a sizeable piece of furniture from a single small piece of precious timber.

These 3mm ($^{1}/_{8}$in) veneers are much less vulnerable to knocks

FAR LEFT: The vacuum press was unable to cope with the tapered oak laminates of this chair's back

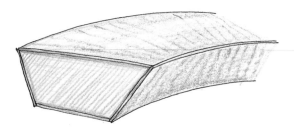

Section of the troublesome cornice and exagererated shape of the veneer segments

ABOVE: The nature of this cornice meant that it could not be veneered by vacuum, and required the use of Scotch glue. The veneer segments needed were of an awkward shape, shown here

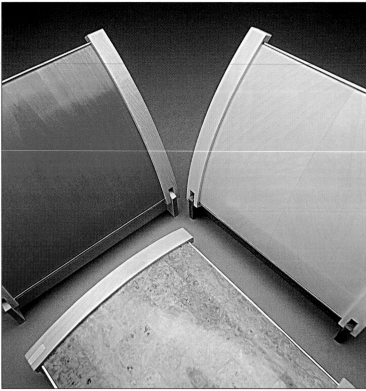

RIGHT: Hot off the press – the lids of these boxes were formed and veneered in the vacuum bag – see F&C No. 4 for construction details

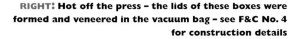

BELOW: This elliptical cupboard makes extensive use of the press, in addition to other techniques

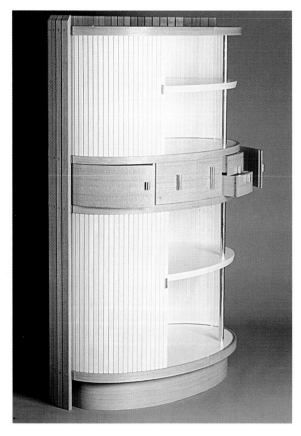

and are more suitable for table tops and so on.

The vacuum press is ideal for gluing workshop-made veneers as the bag will distribute even pressure over the irregularities of the sawing.

The vacuum bag is simply not strong enough to laminate 3mm veneers to small radii, and conventional jigs and band cramps may need to be used. The opportunity should be taken to make some trial pieces and test them to destruction.

I drive a chisel between the laminates; if they show any inclination to part on the glue line I start to worry. The original concert chair was conceived to be made in the vacuum press; this successfully laminated the birch ply with face veneers.

I had always intended the design to be more simple, and attempted a second version with a back made from tapered oak laminates, but the vacuum press was unable to handle them. The next version may involve steam bending the back; but however the design develops, I would never have started it without the vacuum press.

Like any other tool in the workshop the press becomes part of the method of working, opening avenues of design and being employed when it is most appropriate. The elliptical cabinet has ribs laminated from solid oak with a band cramp, shelves veneered with sycamore in the vacuum press and drawer fronts laminated from 1.5mm

($^1/_{16}$in) oak veneers over moulds in the vacuum press.

Back to beginning

Eventually a time comes when none of these sophisticated techniques will work. I was stumped by a simple curved and bevelled cornice that needed crossbanding. Perhaps I shouldn't have designed it, as in the end I had to resort to that messy, wet technique of hand veneering with Scotch glue.

In this instance, as in many others, this age old technique – the avoidance of which had first prompted me to get a vacuum press – had to be the 'state of the art' technology.

Going too far?

The potential of the vacuum press is enormous, but visualising and planning a piece of furniture which is not based on the straight line or circle may involve making complicated drawings or resorting to full-size mock ups and trial and error.

'Undrawable' constructions can be designed, stretched, squeezed and manipulated on a computer which will also produce full-size patterns for each part. For many woodworkers CAD is well beyond the point of no return – for others, it may well be just the beginning. ∎

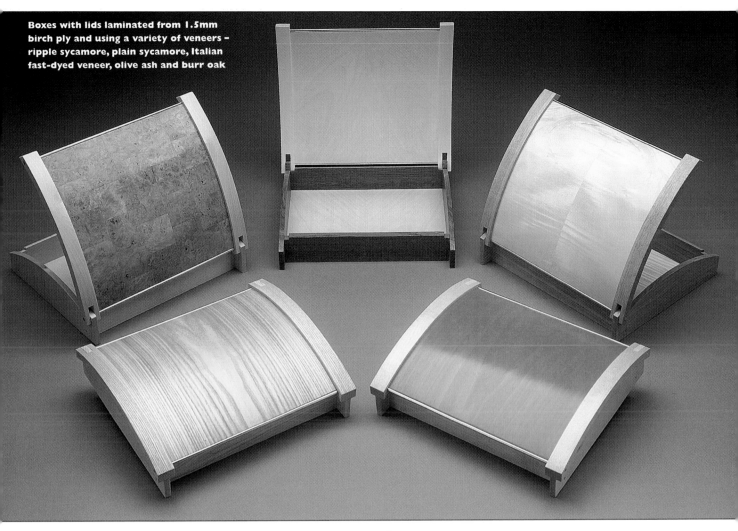

Boxes with lids laminated from 1.5mm birch ply and using a variety of veneers – ripple sycamore, plain sycamore, Italian fast-dyed veneer, olive ash and burr oak

Pressing issues

In part two of his argument in favour of using a vacuum bag when veneering and laminating, **Andrew Skelton** counts the cost

THE TECHNIQUES of veneering and laminating are many and varied, with few rights and wrongs, no secrets or mysteries. Basic common sense, a healthy scepticism and the inquisitiveness to test each method to destruction are the only ways to learn, each new situation being tackled on its merits.

In the first of these two articles I looked at the potential of the vacuum press to expand the scope of the workshop – and its limitations.

I am now turning to the processes of laminating and veneering, not to explain techniques but to look at the costs in terms of equipment, materials and time spent in using the vacuum press.

In my workshop veneering is an expensive process, to be used for its own sake rather than for economy. There is no doubt that in a medium-sized shop with repetitive processes the vacuum bag may represent a very cheap way of achieving results.

In the small shop, where most things are one-offs and machines and operatives are non-specialised, there is little that can be done to achieve these economies.

Moulds

Flat work needs only simple cauls, but for curved work forms must be made. These may be simply shaped from the thickness

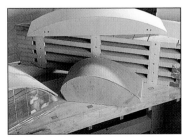

ABOVE: Assorted moulds

of MDF, or whatever, but deeper curves will require moulds to be built up from 'ribs'.

The moulds need to be quite strong so that they don't collapse under pressure, and to present a fair and even surface as irregularities will show through in the finished piece.

ABOVE: **MDF and lippings**

RIGHT: **Approximate bends – 1.5mm cross-grain birch
ply, 3mm MDF and 3mm bandsawn and thicknessed oak**

ABOVE: **Taped
veneers, shooting
board and
Sellotape**

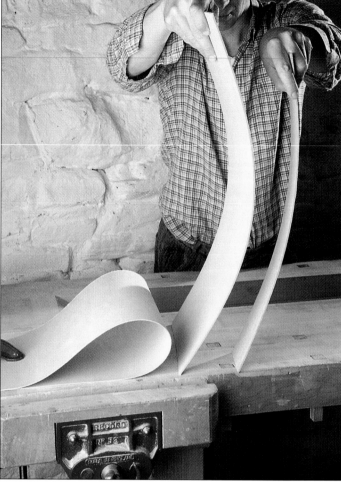

I usually make a thin MDF template, using it to mark out and rout identical ribs. Registration marks help with assembly and alignment. The ribs can be screwed together – say 18mm ($^3/_4$in) ribs and 25mm (1in) gaps – and then covered with several layers of thin hardboard which is contact glued and pinned down, the final layer being glued on in the vacuum bag to avoid pins marking the finished work.

Substrates

Both MDF and plywood are suitable for veneering and are both relatively cheap. MDF is heavier and ply is probably stronger but, of course, will spelch if not cut carefully across the grain.

To protect vulnerable edges and to allow mouldings to be worked before veneering, in most cases the substrate will need lipping. Although many butt glue the lippings I, perhaps pedantically, like to groove the substrate and tongue the lipping.

Ideally I would like to use a tapered tongue but lack the equipment, *see drawing*. If the piece has curved edges lippings need either to be laminated or to have sufficient width to allow the curve to be sawn.

Making, mitring and gluing the lippings is a time-consuming business and, of course, they need carefully cleaning flush with the board before they are veneered over.

Plywood choice

Special bending plywoods are available but I tend to use 1.5mm ($^1/_{16}$in) and 3mm ($^1/_8$in) birch ply and 3mm ($^1/_8$in) and 4mm ($^5/_{32}$in) MDF. Thinner, 2mm ($^5/_{64}$in) MDF, used by picture framers as backs, is sometimes useful.

Bent across the grain, 1.5mm plywood is supple enough for very tight curves, two or three layers making an incredibly strong package. MDF may give a better surface, however. It can be strengthened, if necessary, by alternation with layers of ply.

Veneers

Veneer ranges from 60p to £5 or more per sqare foot, but buying a bundle works out cheaper; however, when you've got ash veneers in stock the customer wants a job in sycamore.

In general both sides of a panel need to be veneered to balance movement; although a cheap 'backing' veneer can be used, employment of the 'face' veneer on both sides is often more appropriate.

Veneers rarely come in the right sizes, so even when not required for a complicated pattern they must be matched, cut and taped.

Commercially, whole bundles of veneers are guillotined and stitched together with a machine that uses a glue 'thread'. In the workshop these have to be cut with a knife and shot between boards with a sharp plane. I use Sellotape as, unlike paper veneer tape, it doesn't need wetting, sticks instantly and reveals the join.

Begin by taping across the join to pull it up, then tape right along it to make sure it stays together.

Choose the tape with care. I once taped up a pile of veneers only to find that the tape had lost its holding power a few hours later with the heat of a summer's day. On the other hand too good a stick will mean resorting to thinners to remove

ABOVE: UF resin, hardener, glue roller and wax

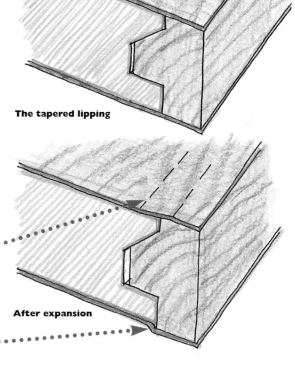

The tapered lipping

Expansion of lipping gives gradual rise of veneereed surface ● ● ● ● ● ●

After expansion

Expansion of lipping results in bump in veneer ● ● ● ● ● ● ● ● ● ● ●

ABOVE: The virtues of a tapered lipping

"When you've got ash veneers in stock the customer wants a job in sycamore"

the pressed tape, to prevent chunks of veneer being stripped away as it is pulled off.

Gluing

Many types and brands of glue may be used for both veneering and laminating – epoxies, urea formaldehyde (UF) resins and PVAs. I mostly use two-part UF resins as they have short pressing times and water clean-up.

Unfortunately the resin, which comes only in 25kg tubs, has an official shelf life of only three months – in practice this can be doubled.

The hardener, which comes only in 25kg sacks, has a much longer life; as it is used in the ratio of 1:5 it will outlast many tubs of resin.

The initial outlay for resin and hardener may be £70. Please note, however, that worries over both health and the environment accompany the use of formaldehyde.

At 15°C – for a flat panel using chipboard as the substrate – this glue will cure in 90 minutes, and at 20°C in 45 minutes, which at least minimises the input of another expensive ingredient of pressing – heat.

I have sited my press in the warmest part of the workshop – upstairs above the stove – and like to stoke up a reasonable heat as I am frankly nervous about pressing with any glue below 18°C.

Anti epoxies

I try to avoid using epoxies as they are difficult to clean up and will stick anything and everything – including the vacuum bag – but in some instances their strength and lack of moisture content make them the only option.

Many workshops use PVAs with great success, but I find that thinly spread it goes off before I am ready and yet needs relatively long pressing times. I'm sure the perfect glue is out there – I just haven't been able to find it.

A job requiring nine laminates and two veneers calls for a glue roller with a hopper. The glue roller – my old model cost about £80 – distributes an even film of glue over the substrate, but don't be too over-zealous or glue will bleed through and ruin the veneers.

Clean up the roller with plenty of hot water as soon as possible after use.

Cauls

With sawn veneers of uneven thickness the veneer may have to be pressed directly by the bag; but use of a caul which both stops the bag becoming covered in glue and distributes the pressure evenly is to be preferred.

Hardboard is ideal for this; although the bottom caul can be

SPRING-BACK FORMULA

THE MOULDS must be made smaller than the final shape as all laminated sandwiches will spring when taken out of the press. By how much? The formula states: spring-back % = $100(1/n2-1)$ where n is the number of laminates (*Wood Bending Handbook* Minstry of Technology; W.C. Stevens and N. Turner; HMSO, 1970), as far as I know out of print.

Put more simply two laminates will suffer 33.3% spring-back whereas five laminates move only 4%. In practice this calculation is unnecessary – and impossible with a free curve – but with seven laminates make the mould a 'bit' smaller and with three make it 'quite a bit' smaller. Also see Bill Clayden's verification and explanation of the formula, pages 67-69.

> "I like to stoke up a reasonable heat as I am frankly nervous about pressing with any glue below 18°C"

ABOVE: Applying pressure

larger than the piece being veneered the top caul needs to be trimmed to no more than 1mm larger all round and have its corners taken off to protect the bag.

If the top caul overhangs too much it may bow as the vacuum is drawn, with the result that pressure will not be applied evenly. Both top and bottom cauls must be waxed or they will become a permanent part of the piece.

These cauls can, of course, be re-used, but they are invariably too small for the next job.

Pressed

So the substrate has been dimensioned and lipped; the veneers cut, shot and taped; cauls have been made and waxed; glue applied; the whole package put in the press and the workshop heated to something most other workplaces consider an average heat.

In a short time a perfect panel or table top can be taken out of the press, its tape carefully removed and its surface scraped and sanded. The veneers are trimmed back to the lipping or dimensioned on the saw, ensuring that cross-grain cuts are preceded

by scoring the veneer to prevent break-out.

Trimmed, cleaned and in place, most veneered work will need protecting by a hefty layer of lacquer; more easily applied oil and wax polish are, in general, unsuitable.

New horizons

This description of veneering is by no means prescriptive or complete, but I have tried to look realistically at what's involved and to dismiss the assumption that veneering cuts costs. Viewed as a means to an end in it own right, veneering and laminating open up new horizons – particularly using the wonderfully versatile vacuum press.

Starting to finish

Tim Judson introduces a series of articles on hand finishes for furniture

● **TIM JUDSON** trained in cabinetmaking and furniture restoration at the **London College of Furniture**. After working in the UK he moved to **North Carolina, USA**, where he now runs a furniture restoration workshop and undertakes some furniture-making commissions.

ARGUABLY, FEW ASPECTS of furniture-making are liable to raise as many differing opinions as wood finishing – and the wide range of options and hefty doses of technical mystique associated with the subject make it less approachable than most.

There is nothing inherently mysterious or alchemic about wood finishes; however there are often several different ways to achieve very similar results. In this series I will be looking at hand applied finishes; these have big advantages in that they require minimal outlay on equipment and involve low toxicity in their application.

In truth, there is very little that spray finishes can do that can't be achieved by hand. The two main advantages of spraying are speed – both in application and drying – and the ability to apply multiple layers of finish without physically disturbing earlier coats.

> ## "Almost always there is a trade-off between a finish's durability and its attractiveness"

Why finish?
So why do we use finishes at all? All finishes have one thing in common – they provide a surface coating on wood.

This serves to protect bare wood from the ravages of daily use and abuse: dirt, abrasion, oxidation, heat, water, solvents and ultraviolet light damage. Finishes also act as a barrier to moisture transfer, slowing the rate of water vapor exchange in timber, therefore reducing the chance of splits and checking in the wood during seasonal moisture cycles, *see fig 1.*

And of course a finish should visually saturate the surface, enhancing both grain and colour.

Unfortunately, no one finish can be said to do all of these things equally well; almost always there is a trade-off between a finish's durability and its attractiveness.

Add to this equation a series of compromises based on the relative flexibility or brittleness of the material, ease of application, drying and curing time, toxicity and repairability, and the choice becomes even less clear – I will go into these aspects in more detail later in the series, when each type of finish will be looked at individually.

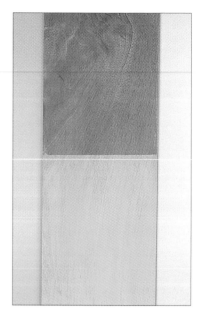

RIGHT: Mahogany
board showing
how a finish can
enhance grain
definition

Balance

Common to all though, is the
importance of applying the finish
uniformly; just as balanced
construction is emphasised during
the making of a piece of furniture, so
should the application of a given
finish be evenly distributed on both
visible and inside faces to avoid
uneven moisture absorption and loss,
one of the prime causes of panel
warping and splits.

This is one area where spray
finishes score in time and
simplicity, as hand finishing often
means pre-finishing work before
assembly, with surfaces to be glued
suitably masked off.

Carcass interiors and framed
panels are both classic examples of
components where special care must
be taken to apply uniform coverage.

Categories

In broad terms, all finishes can be
divided into two categories: either
evaporative or reactive. All contain a
resin of some sort, usually in
conjunction with a solvent; this
solvent acts as a liquid vehicle to
deliver the resin onto the wood.

In the case of evaporative finishes,
all that happens is that the solvent
evaporates to leave behind a resin
film, *see fig 2*. Reapplication of the
solvent will soften the resin and put
it back into solution.

Reactive finishes are defined by

the resin undergoing a chemical
change – either by reacting with
oxygen in the air or with a catalyst –
so that the cured resin is quite
different from its liquid form in the
can. Figure 3 shows how the solvent,
which in this instance is more of a
thinning agent, evaporates; the resin
molecules then reform into the cured
film. After this stage is reached, reapplication of the original solvent
will not dissolve the dry film.

These two categories help to
define how finishes are applied and
how they perform in use.

Evaporative

Evaporative finishes include
shellac, various lacquers such as
nitrocellulose, acrylic, vinyl and so
on, waxes and water-based
emulsion finishes. There are several
advantages to these, not least of
which being the ability of each
application to melt the previous
coat, fusing together to form one
cohesive layer.

There is, therefore, generally
excellent adhesion and lamination
with each previous coat and the
resultant film can be polished to
a high gloss without any of the
interlayer 'witness' lines
sometimes found when rubbing
down reactive finishes.

Additionally, evaporative finishes
are usually easy to repair and blend
with the appropriate solvent.

Reactive

Reactive finishes may consist of
nothing more than resin alone –
examples are raw linseed oil and
tung oil – or include solvents,
metallic driers and other additives as
in the case of oil varnishes.
Polyurethane, alkyd and marine
(phenolic) oil varnishes, Danish oil
and catalyzed lacquers are all
examples of this type.

As it dries, the molecules in the
resin change and combine to form
new, larger macromolecules. Each
application forms a distinct layer

BELOW: Showing
the degree of
colour change
and saturation
effected by
applying a clear
finish

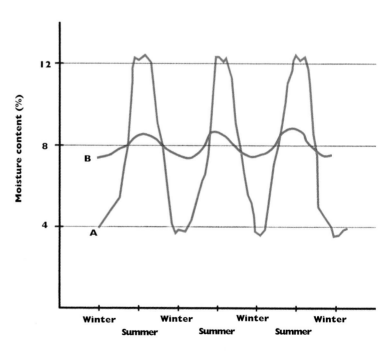

A Unfinished wood stored indoors
B Interior wood with varnish/lacquer finish

ABOVE: Fig 1 Graph showing the difference between the seasonal
shrinkage variation of unsealed and sealed wood

LEFT: As wood is hygroscopic, this kind of shrinkage deterioration can occur after a piece is made unless properly sealed

"A finish should complement the work rather than standing out as a separate entity – integration instead of exhibition!"

and usually requires a sanded 'key' between coats to ensure good mechanical adhesion with previous layers.

As the resin cures there is often a time-limited 'window of opportunity' for additional applications to bond successfully, as with polyurethanes – reading the manufacturer's instructions is definitely a virtue here!

Choosing
The size and intended use of the object to be finished can indicate different choices. It may sound obvious, but a small jewelry box and an oak refectory table will have quite different finish requirements.

Choosing a clear coat finish type usually involves trade-offs, but in many cases different finishes can be used in tandem on a project to provide the advantages of each type; for example, using polyurethane on a table's top and shellac or tung oil on its legs.

Selecting a finish type, therefore, is a decision based on the finish's appearance, durability and the application method involved.

Comparisons
The appearance of a finish is a function of film thickness, clarity and colour. Straight oils – such as tung or linseed – and oil/varnish blends have a characteristic low-build look and will darken the wood's natural tones, enhancing grain definition.

As they do not cure to a hard film, they should not be applied in any great thickness. Shellac, lacquer, varnish and water base are film

finishes; however they can also be applied thinly to give the appearance of oil finishes.

Low build, low molecular weight finishes such as oils are generally more prone to damage but are easier to repair than many film finishes. By contrast, oil-based varnishes, shellac and nitrocellulose lacquers with thicker film build will give good protection against staining and water vapour transfer to the wood.

Water-based finishes fall slightly below cellulose lacquers in terms of protective ability.

Colour
A warm colour tone is produced by all finishes except for light-toned waxes and water-based finishes; these can sometimes look too cool, with none of the amber tones associated with oil based finishes – tinting mediums are often added to water-base to compensate for this.

All finishes containing oil will yellow with age, which can be a

good reason for using water-base on light woods. Combining different finishes, such as an oil coating under shellac to add grain definition, or orange shellac as a base coat to a water-based finish to increase colour warmth, can change and enhance the final result.

However, it is important to check for compatibility between different finish films. Finish clarity here is usually less of a factor – not counting the use of matting agents in satin finishes, which intentionally reduce clarity and gloss.

Dewaxed shellac, lacquer, and oil (alkyd) varnishes give the most transparency, with polyurethanes and water-base producing a more cloudy, artificial appearance.

Wear and tear
Durability affects the degree of protection that the finish imparts to the wood itself, as well as its ability to resist abrasion, heat and water damage.

Almost all reactive crosslinked finishes withstand abuse better than the evaporative solvent-release types, with the exception of oils and oil/varnish blends which, due to their thin builds, are easily marked.

Shellacs and lacquers cure to a brittle film that is easily scratched – this also makes for an easier final rubbing out phase, when abrasives are used to produce varying degrees of gloss sheen.

Oil varnishes produce a softer, but tough, film which resists scratch marking better in use, but they are consequently harder to manipulate with abrasives. Again, more on this subject later.

Context
Finally, it is worth considering the context – does that jewellery box really need a thick gloss varnish protection, or would a satin oil finish be more suitable?

LEFT: The aesthetics of finish choice – different effects obtained from oil varnish and shellac/wax

RIGHT: Selection of brushes for hand-finishing: from left; synthetic bristle for water-base, badger hair for oil varnish, squirrel hair mops for shellac, synthetic bristle and sable pencil brushes for fine work

The aesthetic considerations of wood finishing are just as important as the techniques involved; ideally, a finish should complement the work rather than standing out on the surface as a separate entity – integration instead of exhibition!

However, a reproduction piece will have very different requirements to contemporary design work, so context is critical.

Hand application methods are confined to brushable finishes and those applied with a rag or pad.

Typically they dry and cure more slowly than spray finishes; shellac will dry relatively quickly, but varnishes remain tacky for extended periods. This can affect the amount of dust that settles into the drying film.

While hand-applied finishes need a clean air environment during application, they tend to be more tolerant of humidity and temperature variations than the sprayed variety. They are also relatively cheap and, in some instances, can be made up by the user.

Less material is wasted in overspray, they produce fewer environmental hazards, and consequently are more user-friendly in small work spaces. ■

REFERENCE SOURCES

This series will look at different hand-finish types, and the associated areas of surface preparation, staining and colouring.

This is a vast subject and these articles are intended to be a primer rather than the sum of mankind's knowledge – further reading from the following bibliography is strongly recommended.

Understanding Wood Finishing
by Bob Flexner
Rodale Press, ISBN 0 87596 734 5

Staining and Polishing
by Charles Hayward
Out of print, sometimes available secondhand

Classic Finishing Techniques
by Sam Allen
Sterling, ISBN 0 8069 0513 1

Complete Manual of Wood Finishing
Frederick Oughton
Stobart Davies, ISBN 00 85442 030 4

RIGHT: Fig 2 How an evaporative finish works

FAR RIGHT: Fig 3 How a reactive finish works

solvent   solvent   solvent

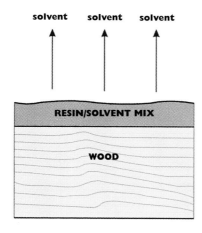

ABOVE: **Evaporative finish during application**

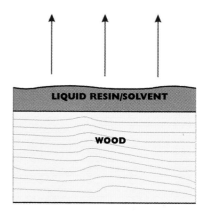

ABOVE: **Reactive finish during application**

BELOW: **Evaporative finish when dry**

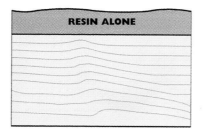

BELOW: **Chemically changed cured resin**

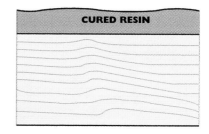

Under the surface

Tim Judson takes a long hard look at preparation in his series on the techniques of hand finishing

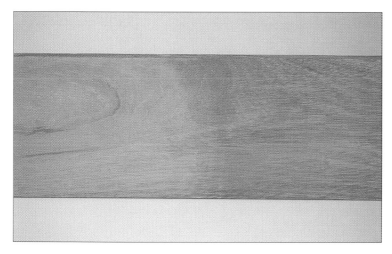

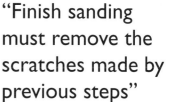

"Finish sanding must remove the scratches made by previous steps"

Sanding can be done either by hand or machine; the main targets are:
a – To remove surface defects
b – To remove scratches left from sanding by using increasingly finer abrasive grits.

This latter involves some discipline. Finish sanding must remove the scratches made by previous steps: 100, 150, 180, or 120, 180, 220, could be useable sequences in power sanding. Below 100 grit is generally reserved for shaping work. If you're sanding by hand, you will need to work through smaller progressions than when power sanding, for example: 80, 120, 150, 180, 220. Remove sanding dust as you progress to clean off coarser abrasive particles left behind.

Generally, softwood can be sanded up to 180 grit; denser woods may need to go to finer grits – boxwood or ebony may require 400 to 600 grits. But a point will be reached when you're only compressing and burnishing wood fibres, which can cause stain and finish absorption problems. Oil finishes will require a finer grit – 220 or more – to produce a tactile, rather than visual, improvement.

NEVER WAS THERE a truer maxim than 'a finish is only as good as the surface preparation'. While it is often viewed as the tedious interlude between the construction of a piece and application of the finish, the quality of the preparatory work often distinguishes a mediocre finish from an excellent one.

Sanding

The two main abrasive materials for use on raw wood are garnet and aluminium oxide. Garnet is a naturally occurring orange-red mineral and provides an excellent abrasive that fractures in use, renewing its surface. Its main drawback is that the abrasive is consequently used up rather quickly.

This friable characteristic makes it the paper of choice for end grain sanding, preventing the burning often found with other abrasives.

Aluminium oxide is a synthetic abrasive, tougher than garnet, and is generally tan in colour. Starting with coarse grits around 40, it progresses to finer grits up to 600 and beyond.

Silicone carbide abrasive is generally reserved for sanding finishes, although it can be used on raw wood. This is available either as regular wet and dry paper or with a metallic soap lubricant added, in this form known as stearated paper or 'Lubrisil'. The white powder lubricant is designed to prevent heat build-up which clogs the paper with finish resin corns.

"A point will be reached when you're only compressing and burnishing wood fibres, which can cause stain and finish absorption problems"

ABOVE LEFT:
Machine sanded wood will appear lighter and show less grain clarity than hand planed wood

LEFT: Power sanding equipment, left to right: palm sander, orbital sander, belt sander

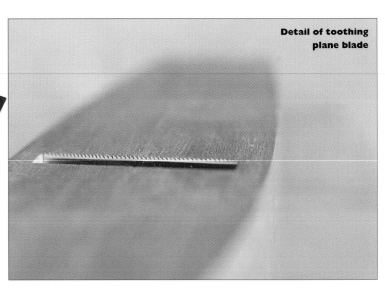

Detail of toothing plane blade

RIGHT: Power sanding defects will be highlighted during staining and finishing

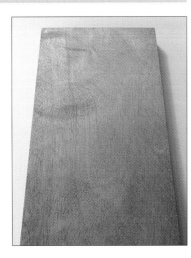

BELOW: Tooled finish equipment left to right: scraper plane, 080 cabinet scraper, Norris A5 smoothing plane, assorted cabinet scrapers

"Slight imperfections – and they should only be slight! – can be part of the character of the surface"

Hand sanding

Hand sanding is more benign in the scratch pattern than that produced by using power tools, but is considerably slower. Usually backed up by a rectangular cork block, the paper is worked exclusively with the grain direction. Taking a standard sheet of sandpaper, cut it lengthwise into thirds then fold it in half again for use with a cork block – giving three fresh faces as you turn the paper – or into thirds again if using by hand alone, *see photos*. Hand sanding is an invaluable technique in tight areas or when sanding smaller components – power sanders have a tendency to round over edges on small stock.

Smoothing

Smoothing, or tooled finishing, involves the use of edge tools rather than abrasives to produce a smooth surface. The idea is to remove machining marks and blemishes using fine-set smoothing planes and scrapers. The plane should be set with a very slightly radiused blade so as not to leave ridge marks. A variety of scrapers can then be used to further level and refine the surface. In some instances, finish can be applied at this point; the slight imperfections – and they should only be slight! – can be part of the character of the piece. Antique furniture often displays these tooled surfaces. However, I find that additional light hand-sanding with 180 grit and upwards will improve the surface.

Overall, tooled finishes offer some distinct advantages over power sanding; they are frequently quicker at levelling than working through progressive abrasive grits and produce a clearer visual surface due to their cutting, rather than abrasive, action. Volume production work will generally require a full sanded approach, trading some degree of quality for speed.

Tooled surfaces are invaluable on ring-porous hardwoods such as ash, oak and elm, which often suffer compression rebound if heavily sanded – the softer early-wood sections get compressed in the attempt to level the harder late-wood areas. When a finish or stain hits this ostensibly flat surface, the varying densities of wood can spring back unevenly, producing a lumpy surface. By cutting rather than abrading, this problem can be avoided.

"With experience, you can locate dips and ridges more readily as a tactile process – in fact your fingers can be one of the most useful finishing tools you possess"

BELOW: Toothing plane

Machine sanding

Machine sanding involves the use of belt sanders, orbital sanders and random orbit sanders. Suffice to say that each type produces a characteristic abrasive pattern which must be eliminated by successive grit sanding to avoid showing under finishes. I find that the hand-held belt sander is the trickiest tool to produce good results with – often as much time can be spent remedying accidental damage as in refining a surface. Special care must be taken when power sanding veneers in this age of skimpy-thin materials.

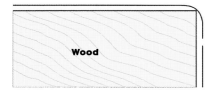

Wood

Surface tension reduces finish thickness on edges

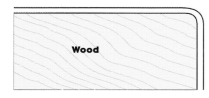

Wood

Rounded edge increases film thickness

ABOVE: Rounding arrises can improve finish coverage due to the surface tension of the liquid film finish

ABOVE: Hand sanding: cork block with sandpaper cut in thirds centre, folded in half for use with block left, folded in thirds again for use alone, right

An 080 cabinet scraper in use

Hand cabinet scraper in use

SANDING PAPERS

The design of sanding papers is important, involving the material to be sanded, the speed of the abrasive action, the flexibility of the backing paper, the life of the abrasive medium and, of course, the cost.

European, Japanese and US grit size grading systems can vary greatly. Broadly speaking European P grades and US CAM I grades are roughly equivalent up to 220 grit. Above that, European grades use higher numbers – a P 800 grit is roughly equivalent to a US 400 grit. The numbers in this article refer to European grades.

As always, sanding involves significant health hazards – adequate breathing filtration is essential, particularly when sanding with power tools.

One method which I find invaluable is to check the surface in a raking light to spot blemishes – particularly on light coloured woods, an overhead light source will make defects almost impossible to see. Use a single light from different angles across the panel for best effect. Fingers can often be more adept than eyes at finding faults – both on raw wood and on finishes. With experience, you can locate dips and ridges more readily as a tactile process – in fact your fingers can be one of the most useful finishing tools you possess.

"One method which I find invaluable is to check the surface in a raking light to spot blemishes'

Edges
Remember to sand the arris, or corner between face and edge, preferably by hand; if an arris is left too sharp, finish films will not cover it adequately, *see diagrams*, due to surface tension in the liquid finish. Sensitive treatment of arrises can really make or break a project – over-sanded mouldings, corners or chamfers can look blunted without the appropriate crispness and definition. This can be a fine line to tread.

Glue residues
One perennial problem with preparing wood for finishing is the removal of glue residues. Dried glue can prevent stain and finish penetration and produce lighter coloured patches. One strategy is to prevent their occurrence in the first place. Avoid using excessive glue during assembly – minimal squeeze-out is sufficient.

TOP: **Hand sanding is often preferable on edges to avoid over-rounded surfaces**

RIGHT: **Glue residues will show up as lighter patches under stains and finishes**

To remove glue, you can either wash it off with hot water while it is still wet or scrape it off when it is dry. Re-sand any washed areas to ensure even stain penetration – otherwise the wetted wood sections will appear darker after staining. If you scrape off dry glue residues, you'll have to take care to remove all glue out of the pores. Acetone or lacquer thinner will help remove dry PVA, especially in conjunction with a wire brush.

Defects

One tool I use on sections of bad tear-out or interlocked grain is a toothing plane. Originally designed as a levelling plane and to provide a key for veneered surfaces, it can be used in a scratch pattern, worked in all directions over the tear-out, which in turn can be quickly cabinet-scraped to a smooth surface. This can avoid over-scraping a defect, resulting in a dip. Another useful technique is to use back bevels on plane irons.

Other potential defects include dents and gouges. Dents are compressed wood fibres – these can be swelled with hot water or steam. Apply water drops with a syringe and heat with an unplugged soldering iron or similar to swell the fibres. Allow to dry thoroughly

BELOW:
Assortment of wood filling materials left to right : pigmented soft wax sticks with spatula tools, tins of coloured wood filler, hard shellac sticks with electric iron tool and alcohol lamp

TOP: **One method for removing dents in wood: first apply water to dent with a dropper...**

ABOVE: **...Then apply heat to dented area with an unplugged iron to produce steam and expand wood fibres**

before sanding the raised grain. Alternatively, use a wetted cloth with the heated iron to introduce steam into the dent. If the wood fibres have been severed, the gouge will have to be filled with either a solid wood patch let into the damage or, for smaller gaps and splits, wood filler.

Repairs using solid wood or veneers will generally be easier to disguise in the finishing process, but graining techniques can be very effective with fillers. These can be a simple mix of glue and fine sawdust – use the minimal amount of glue to avoid a dark patch – or

proprietary fillers are available. These latter have different binders – either lacquer, gypsum or acrylic – and are applied with a spatula, filling slightly proud to allow for shrinkage. Once completely dry, sand level with a flat block. Fillers can be pre-coloured with universal tints, or grained and textured during the finishing process. Over time, however, even the best-matched filler will show as the surrounding wood oxidises and changes colour. Very small pin or nail holes are best filled with soft coloured wax after completing the finishing process. ■

STAINING

Planed or scraped surfaces absorb stains less than sanded surfaces. If staining is a part of the finish procedure, ensure that the surface is entirely worked with cutting tools, or finish sand to the same grit throughout, to avoid uneven colouring. If stains are going to be applied which might raise the wood grain, for example water or alcohol based, it is best to wet the sanded wood surface, allow to thoroughly dry and then lightly finger-sand with 220 grit paper, or finer, to remove raised grain nibs.

Colouring up

In the third part of his series on hand finishing **Tim Judson** looks at staining and colouring

MAIN PICTURE: Wood-stains require top-coating to produce the final colour. The stain alone, left, and with finish applied, right

ABOVE: Dye-stains have fully dissolved colourants, left, while pigmented-stains have particles which require stirring to produce the stain colour evenly, right

> "Stains can include liquids and gels applied to raw wood, or glazes and toners which are applied in, or between, coats of finish"

T HE PROCESS OF colouring wood is often associated with the production of cheap furniture where it is used to hide poor workmanship and low quality materials.

In a well made piece, with carefully selected wood, colouring is often quite unnecessary, although, when it is used with finesse, it can enhance the work either by blending natural colour mis-matches, or simply by adding a rich and vibrant look to the surface.

> "Altering the natural colour of wood involves the use of stains to add colour, as well as bleaches to remove it"

The basics

Colouring wood is a large subject, and I can only touch on the basics here – the bibliography in the first article of this series is a useful reference point for additional information, *see page 88*.

Altering the natural colour of wood involves the use of stains to add colour, as well as bleaches to remove it. Stains can include liquids and gels applied to raw wood, or glazes and toners which are applied in, or between, coats of finish.

The difference between these materials is in the sequence in which they are applied during the finishing process.

Stain types

A simple way to understand stains is to divide them into categories; although there are large numbers of different products available, they all divide into three groups – pigmented, chemical, *see panel*, and aniline dye stains.

Pigments are finely ground, opaque mineral particles which obscure the natural colour of the wood – a heavy concentration, such as in paint, will totally obscure the wood grain.

In stains, these pigment particles are dispersed in a solvent and a binder.

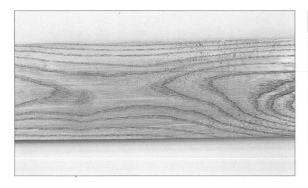

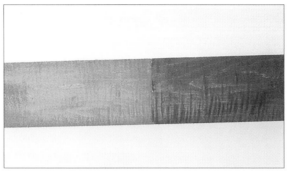

> "Dyes are crystals which dissolve into tiny particles called ions, so small that they appear transparent. Their electro-chemical structure, or polarity, gives them a strong bonding affinity with wood"

TOP: Pigment-stains will emphasise grain and large pores, as on this section of ash

ABOVE: Pigment-stains will obscure grain definition, as on this curly maple, left, dye-stains will emphasise grain figure, right

BELOW LEFT: Dyes should be applied liberally on the surface...

BELOW RIGHT: ... before removing excess with a rag

When applied to a wood surface, the particles lodge in crevices in the wood structure – the larger the pore size, the more pigment will collect. To some degree, pigmented stains can also build on top of the wood surface, when applied heavily enough.

The purpose of the binder is to lock the particles onto the surface after the solvent evaporates. Although the binder is typically either oil, varnish, lacquer, or water-based, in most cases it is easier to note the solvent type used in the stain: white spirit, alcohol, lacquer-thinner, or water.

Dyes

Dyes are much smaller, molecular-sized particles, unlike pigments which colour the wood by lying on the surface, dyes saturate the wood fibre structure. Consequently they do not require a binder to hold them onto the surface, only a solvent to deliver them into the wood fibres.

Dyes are crystals which dissolve into tiny particles called ions, so small that they appear transparent. Their electro-chemical structure, or polarity, gives them a strong bonding affinity with wood.

Unlike pigmented stains with a binder – polymeric stains – dyes must be top-coated to saturate the colour. The transparency of the medium produces a totally different effect on the wood. On highly figured wood such as ripple sycamore, a dye will enhance the quilted figure where a pigment would obscure it; on a strongly grained wood, such as ash, a dye would give a fairly even tone overall, where a pigment stain would emphasise the contrast in the grain lines.

Likewise on endgrain, a dye stain will give lighter, more even tones than pigments.

Compatibility

The choice of solvent or binder will not affect the final colour produced, but the chosen stain should be compatible with the clear finish to be used.

If the solvent is alcohol, with lacquer-thinner or water in both the stain and finish, there may be an adverse reaction between the two.

If the solvent is white spirit, in either the stain or the finish, you will avoid any compatibility problems – with the exception of applying oil or varnish over an oil-based stain.

Reactions are almost invariably caused by applying incompatible finishes over stains with a brush or rag – which highlights one big advantage of spray-applied finishes!

Vehicle

The most common vehicle for pigment stain has been, up until recently, oil thinned with white spirit.

Varying the ratios of pigment to

binder and solvent produces anything from artist's tube paints, with almost no solvent, to Japan colours, with metal salts added to speed drying, to commercial D.I.Y. stains which have added white spirit. Thickening materials can be added to produce wiping and gel stains.

Recently, water-based pigmented stains have become a low-toxicity alternative to the oil-based forms, and are compatible with almost all finishes.

Light-fast

Pigments are generally more fade resistant, or light-fast, than dyes. Dyes are soluble in oil, lacquer thinner, alcohol, or water, and come either as a powder or premixed.

Alcohol-soluble dyes are probably the most problematic due to their fast drying time, which can result in lap-marks, or dark streaks – and their relatively poor fade-resistance.

Water-aniline dyes penetrate the deepest and are the most light-fast – and they avoid the problems of lap-marking, flammability and toxicity.

Application

Applying a stain is simplicity itself – flood it on and wipe it off before it dries.

Virtually anything can be used as an applicator – a rag, brush, sponge, or spray gun.

Applying generously will help to keep the whole surface wet and avoid lap-marks.

Pigmented stains will be lighter the more you wipe off, and each successive application will add more colour and obscure more grain.

Dye stains can be darkened by adding more powder to the mix and lightened with more solvent.

As a rule, wait until the first coat is dry before re-staining; with dye stains, additional applications of the same mix will not generally change the final dry result.

Gelled pigment stains are a new addition and tend to penetrate less than ordinary liquid stains. They excel on woods that absorb liquid stains unevenly, such as cherry and pine, as the gel causes the pigment to lie evenly over the surface.

ABOVE LEFT: Glazes, or Japan colours, are thick pigment suspensions which can be thinned to the desired consistency

ABOVE: Sample board: lightly stained wood 1, seal-coat applied 2, glaze and second sealer applied to add more character and age 3

BELOW: Sponge brushes make good stain applicators, with more control than rags

MIXING COLOURS

Sometimes you can find just the colour you want straight from a can, but when you can't, you can either combine different proprietary stains, or mix your own.

If you keep to the same solvent type there should be no problem – avoid mixing oil with water, or dyes with pigments. Stains of the same type, even from different manufacturers, can be mixed at will. If in doubt about compatibility stick to the same brand in a manufacturer's line.

Dye-stains can be purchased as dry powders and mixed with the appropriate solvent – alcohol, white spirit or lacquer thinner, or water – typically at 1 oz. powder to 1 quart solvent, in a non-metallic container.

I recommend warm distilled water for mixing water-based stains as the minerals in tap water can alter the final colour.

Straining the dye mixture after several hours will remove undissolved powder.

Blending colours

A whole book could be written about colour theory – and a lot can be learnt by simple experimentation with different stains – but some points to remember are:
– Complimentary colours will neutralise or subdue each other.
– Useful pairs are blue and orange, red and green, and purple and yellow – if your stain is too red, add some green; too orange, add some blue and so on. Earth tones can be used in the same way – a cool greenish raw umber will tone down the red in burnt sienna.
– Earth pigments are generally much more useful as colourants than pure colours.
– Black added to any colour will reduce its intensity and, added to orange, will produce brown – probably the most useful colour in wood finishing.

RIGHT: Carved and sealed pillar without glaze

FAR RIGHT: Adding glaze and wiping off top surfaces can enhance the carving definition

"Stain can often look rather flat when used alone, so additional colours can be added on top of seal-coats to increase the appearance of depth"

Shading, toning and glazing

In addition to straight stains, wood can be coloured by using pigments and dyes to shade, tone, and glaze during the finishing process.

Stain can often look rather flat when used alone, so additional colours can be added on top of seal-coats to increase the appearance of depth.

One trick is to use a dye-stain under a pigment-stain to emphasise different parts of the wood structure.

Pigments can be used between layers of finish, or glazing, to add graining and character to bland wood, or to give an antique look, with darker material in the recesses,

BELOW: A/B wood bleaches can alter wood colours – black walnut can be changed to a lighter tone, left, rosewood will lose colourants more selectively, right, – and some interesting results can be produced on tropical hardwoods

as in carved or turned work. These are normally Japan colours which are manipulated while still wet to produce a variety of different possible effects.

Avoid applying too thickly and over-finishing while the previous coat is not completely dry – both these things can cause the top-finish coats to peel.

Pickling, or limed finishes are similar – instead of dark glaze colours, light pigment paints are used instead.

Dyes can be used in clear finishes to add tinting colours, which will shade and blend varying wood tones. Spray application works best with this, although I have used both polishing rubbers and brushes to good effect.

Bleaching

Colouring wood can involve the selective removal of colours with bleaches. There are three types of wood-bleaches:

– Oxalic acid, which removes iron and water stains, as well as weathered silvering on exterior wood.

– Chlorine bleach, which is often available as swimming pool bleach made up of calcium and sodium hypochlorite, is effective only on dye stains. It can remove an aniline stain without lightening the natural wood colours.

– Two-part bleach, known as A/B bleach, contains both a strong alkali and an acid-hydrogen peroxide, which are often applied separately, but work together on the surface to lighten natural wood colours as well as neutralise dyes and pigments. It leaves no crystalline residue when dry, unlike the other two. Neutralise this A/B bleach with a mild acid, such as vinegar and water, and rinse chlorine and oxalic acid bleach residues with plenty of water.

Natural wood colourants will not all bleach out uniformly – this fact can be used to produce some interesting results through experimentation! ∎

METAMERISM

One factor that is seldom mentioned in finish colouring is metamerism – the capacity for colours to change under different light sources. Check your colour works under the light source that it will be displayed in, be it incandescent, fluorescent, or daylight.

Watery finish

Tim Judson looks at water-base finish in his series on the techniques of hand finishing

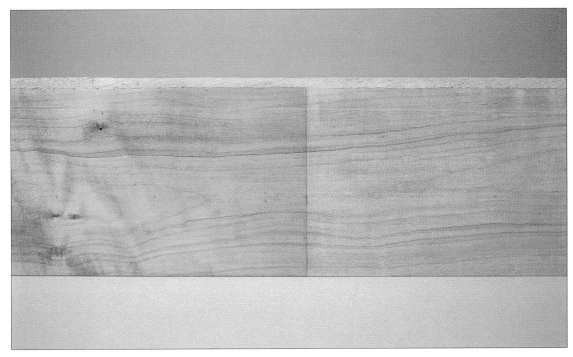

LEFT: Contrast between water-based acrylic finish on maple board, right, with warmer colour of orange shellac, left

ENVIRONMENTALISM IS A watchword of today, and water-based finishes are one way in which woodworking can respond to it. Water-based finishes are emulsions, a chemistry they share with white and yellow glues as well as latex paints. The high content of water in emulsions allows the toxic solvent content to be greatly reduced, but not eliminated, relative to other traditional finishes – which greatly reduces flammability. This accounts for their marketing as safe finishes.

> "Water-based finishes are emulsions, a chemistry they share with white and yellow glues as well as latex paints"

Low toxicity

The main advantage of water-based finishes is their lower toxicity, both in application and disposal. Despite earlier problems, most water-based finishes today have improved formulations that reduce grain raising and improve adhesion between coats. They are reasonably easy to use, quick drying, simple to clean up, and do not require explosion-proof ventilation when sprayed. They are scuff-resistant and will not yellow – an advantage with some woods and limed colour finishes. However, there are still marked differences in appearance and durability between different brands. I suggest some experimentation between various brands, not least because many are formulated for specific uses such as spray-only application – more so than with traditional finishing materials.

Make-up

Water-based finishes are coalescent finishes, bridging the gap between reactive and evaporative finishes.

> "They are reasonably easy to use, quick drying, simple to clean up, and do not require explosion-proof ventilation when sprayed"

They consist of a resin, usually acrylic or polyurethane, which is dispersed in water as tiny cured droplets. These two elements are chemically incompatible, so bridging solvents and surfactants are added to combine the resin in the water and form the emulsion. The water evaporates when the finish is applied, whereupon glycol ether 'tail solvents', which evaporate more slowly than water, soften the resin droplets, allowing the droplets to combine and fuse into a cohesive

"Never sand water-based finishes between coats with wire wool"

film, *see diagrams*. These solvents are present in small quantities which accounts for the reduced overall toxicity. The full formulation is complex relative to oil varnishes and lacquers, and includes soaps to reduce surface tension, de-foamers, flow-out additives, flatting agents and, in some cases, catalysts to crosslink the resin to a more durable film, closer to a polyurethane macromolecule structure. Because these proportions are carefully balanced, it is inadvisable to thin the finish more than about 10-20%.

Application
It must be said that water-based finishes are the most difficult to apply of the common wood finishes. Because of the water content, they have a tendency to raise the grain. One solution is to sponge the raw wood and sand the fibres before application. Alternatively, a wash-coat of de-waxed shellac can be used to seal the grain. Water-base will bond well to shellac if it is scuff-sanded first, and the shellac will add colour to the wood surface. A thin coat of water-based sanding sealer is another option, sanding smooth when dry.

Never sand water-based finishes between coats with wire wool – tiny metal residues can rust, forming black spots in the finish. Synthetic wire wool is a suitable alternative, or use silicone carbide paper.

Brushes and brushing
Most water-based finishes are supplied at brushing consistency. Use a good quality synthetic – nylon or nylon blend – brush with tapered bristles to reduce air bubbles. Natural bristles will swell in water and splay their bristles. Wet the brush in distilled water – minerals in hard tap water can mark the finish with small sand-like specks – before loading the brush with finish, as with standard varnish.

Holding the brush at about a 30° angle to the surface, apply the finish in long, steady strokes. Avoid back-brushing or attempts to brush out air bubbles – these will pop before the finish dries. Thin coats are better than thick ones, especially on vertical surfaces where runs can form. Note that water-based finishes have a high resin content relative to other finishes. As with oil varnishes, dried runs can be carefully chiselled or scraped level.

ABOVE: Water-based emulsion finishes appear as a cloudy white liquid in the can
BELOW: During application, the finish has a whitish/purple appearance that dries to a clear transparent coating

LEFT: Sanding between coats will improve intercoat adhesion

"If the weather is humid, try increasing airflow over the work with a fan – but preferably wait for a drier day"

Drying

Water-base finishes will dry quickly – touch-dry in 10-15 minutes and re-coat in about 1½ hours. On large projects, this quick drying can cause problems in covering the whole area in one shot. Try working sections at a time and maintain a 'wet edge' between each section using extenders, usually propylene glycol, which can be added to slow the water's evaporation. 1 oz. to one gallon is about right, but check the manufacturer's recommendations.

"Holding the brush at about a 30° angle to the surface, apply the finish in long, steady strokes"

After the coat is dry, scuff sand with fine sandpaper before applying the next coat. Remove sanding dust with a damp cloth or compressed air, but avoid oiled tack cloths, as they can cause problems with finish adhesion. If subsequent finish-coats pull into ridges, this can be a sign of oil contamination from a tack cloth or silicone. Remove the application with wet cloths, or paint stripper if it has dried; wash down with naphtha and seal in the oil with de-waxed shellac, preferably sprayed, before proceeding with water-base coats. I strongly advise against using fisheye eliminators – these contain silicone oil and only fight fire with fire. They can and do contaminate everything in your finishing area!

Problems

Other specific problems include foaming of the finish during brushing, caused by agitating the surfactant (soap) which creates the emulsion in the finish. The addition of a small amount of white spirit, 1 oz./1 gallon, can help to eliminate this. Check that your finish is actually formulated for brushing.

Temperature and humidity can be problematic, due to the water content. Water-bases have less tolerance for high humidity, above 80% R.H., and temperatures outside of 15-25 C. Adding distilled water, 10-15%, or propylene glycol, as mentioned above, during hot or dry conditions will slow the drying and help the finish flow out. If the weather is humid, try increasing airflow over the work with a fan – but preferably wait for a drier day.

Intercoat adhesion

Poor intercoat adhesion is another problem with water-base, these show up as faint ring-shaped lines, or 'witness' lines, during sanding or rubbing out and can necessitate wholesale removal of the topcoat. The problem lies in insufficient solvent needed to combine the resin surfaces during the initial set-up. A small addition, again, about 1 oz./1 gallon, of acetone or lacquer thinner will add bite to the wet coat and help each coating to fuse into a continuous film. Because water-based finishes cure by a sequence of water and solvent evaporation, if humidity or temperature extremes upset this sequence it can lead to poor film formation, blushing or blanching, and poor adhesion between coats. Remove the offending layers and reapply. Again, this underscores the need to apply this finish under relatively optimal conditions – the rule of thumb could be: if the weather is uncomfortable for you, it

will also be so for the finish. Never allow stored cans of finish to freeze or even drop down into single digit temperatures – emulsions are destroyed by cold and will not reformulate when warmed.

Compatibility

Water-based finishes have only limited compatibility with other finishes and stains. For example, water-base applied over an oil-based stain can later de-laminate in whole sheets. Water and alcohol soluble aniline dyes and NGR (non-grain raising) stains are fully compatible. Alternatively, use de-waxed shellac as a seal coat over incompatible stains. Water-base dries to a water-clear colour; while this can be an advantage with some light woods, some people prefer the more natural amber tones of oil-based finishes. Try using a base coat of shellac to warm the colour, or add some orange, red or brown water-soluble or NGR dye stain to the finish. Experiment on scrap wood to achieve the degree of colour you want – usually only a small amount is required.

BELOW: Drawings show process of water-based finish curing, from liquid, I, through initial cure, 2, to final cured film, 3

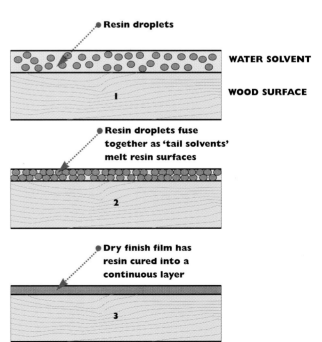

● Resin droplets

WATER SOLVENT

WOOD SURFACE

1

● Resin droplets fuse together as 'tail solvents' melt resin surfaces

2

● Dry finish film has resin cured into a continuous layer

3

Although this article is not about spraying, I should sound a note of warning: during spraying, the resin droplets become thoroughly atomised. As these uncured resin droplets are water wetted and of relatively low volatility compared to spray lacquers, they will stick to the lining of your lungs if inhaled. Consequently, water-base is considerably more toxic compared to traditional spray finishes in this respect, where lacquer particles cure very quickly in overspray – so always use a full-face organic vapour mask in the spray booth. Avoid excessive breathing of water-base fumes and skin contact: although the solvent content is very low, the glycol ether solvents used are toxic in their own right and can cause symptoms of dizziness.

ABOVE: Water-based or NGR dyes can be used to tint water-based finishes

Cleanup

Cleanup is simple: wash brushes in warm soapy water before the finish is dry. However, brush bristles can be ruined if the finish is allowed to dry on them. Acetone, lacquer thinners and paint removers can dissolve the resin, but often at the expense of the brush. Don't dispose of used finish down the sink or drain – you can find yourself the proud owner of well-blocked pipes – tap water minerals can turn finish resins into congealed sticky goo!

Resistance

All water-based finishes have good resistance to scratching and scuff marking. They do not score as high as oil-based polyurethanes in regard to heat and solvent resistance and can water-mark fairly readily. They also provide a poor barrier to water-vapour transmission – although in the case of latex paints, this is often seen as an advantage. To improve the resistance in these areas, some manufacturers supply crosslink hardeners to increase the durability and heat or solvent resistance. These additives tend to be toxic, which undermines the rationale for using water-based finishes in the first place. ■

RIGHT: Applying water-based finish when the temperature is too cold can result in poor flow-out and surface dimpling

Using oil and varnish

Tim Judson looks at oil and oil varnishes in his series on hand finishing

ALTHOUGH SOMETIMES viewed as an inferior finish, oils and varnish are among the most versatile in the hand-applied finish category. Unfortunately, there is considerable confusion between the many types of oil, and oil varnish, finishes available today. Almost all oil-based finishes can be divided into three basic groups: straight oil finishes, oil varnishes, and combinations of these two.

Oil finishes

Straight oil finishes are what their name suggests – unmixed oils extracted from plants, nuts and petroleum. If shellac and cellulose lacquer are examples of film-forming finishes that build on the surface of the wood, then oils are the definitive penetrating finishes, with little or no surface build.

Not all oils are suitable as furniture finishes – the dividing factor being the degree to which they will cure out of a liquid state. Linseed and tung oil will both form solids from reaction with oxygen; others, such as mineral oil, do not absorb oxygen and consequently never cure at all. Those that are suitable as finishes, such as tung and linseed oil, share similar characteristics: they cure slowly and produce a soft finish, so all excess residues must be wiped off during application. They also cure to a satin finish – attempting to achieve a high gloss is inadvisable as the dry film is plastic enough to mark with a fingernail.

Oil varnishes

Oil varnishes include a variety of types such as alkyd, phenolic and polyurethane varnishes. Historically, varnishes were made from natural resins, but today these resins are almost all synthetic; the varnish is made by combining the given resin with oil, under a heated reaction, which chemically changes them both to produce the varnish. Oil varnishes cure much faster than oils alone, and produce a thicker, glossier finish which is resistant to most common damage including scratches, water, stains and moisture vapour exchange in the wood. They are the most durable category in the hand-applied finish range.

> "Oil varnishes include a variety of types such as alkyd, phenolic and polyurethane varnishes"

Oil and varnish blends

Combining oil and varnish produces a finish that takes characteristics from both: the oil content makes the finish cure more slowly, and to a lower sheen than straight varnish alone. It also softens the finish, precluding a high film build. The varnish component gives the film more gloss and toughness than a straight oil would. There is considerable variation in different manufacturer's formulations, altering the ratio of oil to varnish and consequently the nature of the final film produced. As a result, many woodworkers resort to making their own blends. These are often referred to as Danish oil: generally linseed oil cut with a substantial amount of white spirit and with a small amount of an alkyd resin varnish included.

Just to add to the confusion, many manufacturers label their finishes as oil finishes without specifying the ingredients – as a rule of thumb, most of these will be oil and varnish blends.

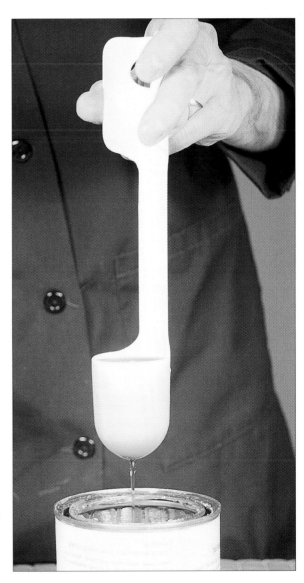

> "Combining oil and varnish produces a finish that takes characteristics from both"

ABOVE: Brush technique for oil varnishes: apply first brush stroke with or across the grain, and in from the edge, with the brush at about 45°...

ABOVE: ...back-brush the second stroke to cover the uncovered edge, so as to prevent drips and runs
BELOW : ...when fully covered, tip-off the excess varnish with the brush held lightly at a near vertical position, brushing with the grain

BELOW : Over-loaded brushes can produce runs along the edges of a board – tap the ferrule inside the can when loading the brush to remove excess varnish

Wiping varnish

A fourth oil-based finish is wiping varnish – this is an ordinary oil varnish thinned with enough white spirit to allow it to be applied with a rag. It isn't really a distinct finish type in its own right, but it is easier to apply than brushing varnish and its high solvent content makes it dry faster.

Applying oils

Linseed and tung oil alone make poor furniture finishes: they provide minimal protection from damage and mark easily. Raw linseed oil can have metallic dryers added to speed the drying – this is known as boiled linseed, but this does not improve its finish qualities. Both these oils will darken over time and provide flexible penetrating finishes. They are best applied slightly warmed, flooded onto the surface and allowed to sink in before wiping off excess material.

Because of the poor performance of straight oils, it is preferable to opt for an oil and varnish blend instead. The prime advantage touted for oil finishes, namely that they are easily repaired, is equally true for oil and varnish blends. These provide somewhat better protection than straight oils against wear, water damage, and the like; however, their main attraction is ease of application as they allow plenty of working time and give an attractive low-build low-gloss sheen; but, they should be avoided for things like table tops that have a lot of wear.

> "Remember that white spirit will not dissolve a reactive oil finish once it is dry"

> "Because of the poor performance of straight oils, it is preferable to opt for an oil and varnish blend instead"

Bleeding

One problem in applying oil and varnish blends involves bleeding out of the wood pores. This occurs more in large pored woods like oak, and is caused by two main factors:
a – The solvent, or white spirit, evaporating and pulling the finish out with it from the pores.
b – The finish expanding out of the pores as the wood heats up from vigorous rubbing, or if the wood is moved from a cold room to a warmer one.

The dried residues can either be abraded off with fine wire or synthetic wool and over-finished again, or the whole removed with proprietary stripper. Remember that white spirit will not dissolve a reactive oil finish once it is dry. This problem tends not to affect wiping varnishes, due to their faster cure rate, or straight oils, as they typically have a low solvent content.

Repairs

Oil finishes can offer simple repairs for scratch damage – merely reapplying will saturate the damage and make it less visible – as will any thinly applied finish. However, they can be difficult to repair if water or heat has discoloured the wood. Water will tend to raise the grain, which can be smoothed with fine sandpaper or 0000 wire wool before applying more finish to even out the sheen. Heat and stain

SPRAYING VARNISH

Because varnish takes so long to dry, it is generally regarded as an excellent brushing finish and a terrible one to spray. One reason for this is that, being slow to dry, sags and runs can easily form; also atomised particles of varnish can settle into the wet film with obvious results!

However, it is possible to spray varnish by thinning it with an appropriate amount of a fast-drying solvent such as naphtha or acetone, and spraying it in light coats at low pressure. An initial misted tie-down coat on vertical surfaces can help bind subsequent coats and reduce sags. Airless spray systems can work well too, and do not require the varnish to be thinned with solvent.

I can't honestly say I recommend spraying varnishes; I've never found the end result to be half as good as an equivalent brushed surface.

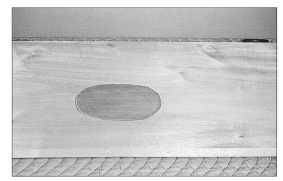

damage may need to be sanded to bare wood before refinishing, or in some cases bleached with oxalic or chlorine bleach. Matching the colour tones back perfectly is usually problematic.

"Varnishes contain different resins which affect their performance"

Applying wiping varnish

The next step up in durability is wiping varnishes – these are thinned ordinary varnishes, usually at a 2:1 ratio of white spirit to varnish, which offer greater protection than oil and varnish blends. Although often sold as oil finishes, the fact that the oil and varnish resins have been heated to produce a different chemical product make them very different to oil blend finishes. Varnishes contain different resins which affect their performance, see below – if a thin build is desired, the particular resin won't matter greatly. However, if you want a thicker build, you might want to thin a specific varnish to tailor your own recipe, which will be considerably cheaper too.

Wiping varnish will build more slowly than brushed varnish due to its thinness; but, varnish's hardness relative to oils gives it greatly superior resistance to scratches and stains. Wiping varnishes are applied with a rag, removing the excess as with oils, and will cure to a hard cohesive film.

"You might want to thin a specific varnish to tailor your own recipe"

Safety warning

An important safety note with these wiped oil finishes: do not dispose of the used rags in a closed space – the oils can spontaneously combust. Spread the rags out singly to allow adequate ventilation until the oils have sufficiently cured.

Identification

It can be very difficult to tell some of these oil and varnish finishes apart, as they tend to look and smell the same. One method is to test for the oil content: apply a small amount on a non-porous surface – if it wrinkles after it cures, it has a high oil content and will be an oil and varnish blend. A smooth surface indicates a wiping or ordinary varnish. The oil and varnish blend film will also be much softer than the varnish and will dry much more slowly.

Applying varnish

Varnishes are available in a variety of formulations and with different resins depending on the required use. Phenolic resins are used in exterior and marine varnishes; they produce a soft flexible film which can accommodate the movement of wood in the outdoors. Alkyd resin is the most commonly used resin in interior varnishes and is also found in lacquers and oil paints. Polyurethane is available in several forms but is frequently modified with alkyd resins to produce a uralkyd varnish. This is the most durable and scratch-resistant of the three resin forms.

All these varnishes cure by absorption of oxygen; typically this process is accelerated by the addition of metallic dryers. As mentioned, varnish is a combination of oil and varnish resins combined with heat. The ratio of oil to resin will affect the final film: high oil content, or long-oil, is found in exterior varnishes where it adds flexibility. Low oil content, or short to medium-oil, produces a harder film for indoor use.

"Alkyd resin is the most commonly used resin in interior varnishes and is also found in lacquers and oil paints"

● Phenolic resins will yellow significantly as they age and are usually combined with tung oil. They can be flexible or, with less oil, can produce a hard high-gloss film suitable for table tops.

● Alkyd resins are not as tough as phenolic, but they are cheaper to produce and won't yellow as much.

● Polyurethanes, in combination with an alkyd, will be the toughest of these three; however, they have a more opaque 'plastic' look, bond very poorly with their cured form, and all other finishes, and will not stand up to sunlight, which makes them peel.

Resistance in varnish

All varnishes have a strong molecular structure which makes them very resistant to heat, water, solvents and abrasion. They greatly slow water vapour exchange in wood, reducing wood movement. Typically they are applied by brush; their slow cure time – 1 hour touch-dry or overnight to re-coat – makes them susceptible to dust settling in the drying film, so a clean working environment is necessary. Varnishes have a high solids content, so two or three coatings is usually sufficient. The first seal coat should be thinned 1:1 with white spirit; subsequent coats can be thinned by 10-20 % to improve brushing qualities. Use a good quality badger bristle brush, or a nylon and polyester blend, with flagged tip bristles; initially wet the brush with white spirit to condition the bristles. Dip the brush no more than halfway into the varnish and tap the excess off on the container side – avoid scraping it off on the side of the can.

Brushing

Apply the varnish in long strokes to deliver a thin, even coat. Too thick a layer and the material will not cure properly – varnish cures from the outside in. It is often helpful to apply by brushing first across the grain before levelling out with the grain. Finally, use the tipping-off technique, shown to remove excess material. Initial application has the brush held at 45° or so. Avoid scrubbing the varnish on the surface with the brush as this can foam the finish with air bubbles. Final tipping off should be done with the brush held almost vertically and the tip dragged very lightly with the grain to remove brush marks and blemishes. Take care to prevent building up ridges and runs around edges. To remove them when dry, use a sharp chisel or scraper.

Sanding between coats

Varnish should be scuff sanded between coats with 220 grit abrasive to give a key between each layer. Take care to remove any bumps and defects – if they are left until the final sanding, you may sand through coats, producing visible ring-like witness lines. Rectifying this requires sanding off the whole top-coat and reapplying. Different varnishes vary, but typically allow 24 hours between coats and a full 72 hours after the final coat before rubbing out.

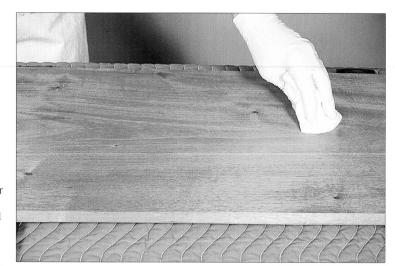

"Use a good quality badger bristle brush, or a nylon and polyester blend, with flagged tip bristles"

Because varnish cures by chemical reaction, warmer temperatures will speed the drying and cold temperatures can retard it drastically – keep a minimum of 15°C. If the weather is very hot, try thinning the varnish with 15 to 20% white spirit to retard the drying and allow the brush marks and air bubbles to flow out. ▧

"I can't honestly say I recommend spraying varnishes; I've never found the end result to be half as good as an equivalent brushed surface"

GRAIN FILLER

Because of the high resin content, varnish can be used as a binder for a grain filler. Collect final sanding wood dust, of 220 grit, from the project in hand, and mix with full-strength varnish to the thickness of honey. Work this paste into the pores across the grain with a putty knife instead of the dilute seal coat, before removing the excess. Allow a day to cure before sanding with 220 grit and applying top coats of varnish.

The maligned Shellac

Tim Judson continues his series on the techniques of hand finishing

LEFT: Various grades of shellac, in both button and flake form

S HELLAC IS PERHAPS the most misunderstood of all finishes. It is also surrounded by the most mystique, notably in the techniques of French polishing. It is a classic evaporative finish with low toxicity – in fact, dry shellac is edible – and it has a wide range of possible uses and application methods. Best of all, it is the most forgiving of all finishes, being so easily repairable – it's almost impossible to get into a situation which can't be readily resolved.

> "It is a classic evaporative finish with low toxicity – in fact, dry shellac is edible!"

Maligned

Much has been said, often erroneously, about shellac's detractions – that it is awkward to use, it is easily marked, it isn't durable, and so forth. However, its strong points are many. Shellac is probably the most attractive finish available; it has excellent resistance to ultra-violet deterioration and darkening, being about the most stable of all natural or synthetic resins. It is tough enough to be used as a floor finish, making it also a superb 'tie-down' or seal coat with good bonding to most other finishes. It can seal over knots, oils and waxes, is easy to repair and has excellent resistance to moisture vapour transmission.

It is the most frequent choice for restoration of antique surfaces as well as being an excellent finish for modern furniture.

Admittedly it does have a few shortcomings in that it readily re-dissolves in alcohol – but in many ways, this is an advantage in terms of repair – and it will heat-mark above 180°F.

> "It can seal over knots, oils and waxes, is easy to repair and has excellent resistance to moisture vapour transmission"

Origins

As a finishing material in the West, shellac came to prominence in the 1820's with the advent of French polishing and industrial refining of shellac.

Derived from the raw material known as 'stick-lac', shellac is available in several grades of dry shellac, either in flake or button form, and in various colours.

Dry shellac flakes will have an indefinite shelf life if kept stored cool and dry. 'Seedlac' is a dark red colour, and is the

RIGHT: Wax
settling out as
a cloudy film
when left to
stand

FAR RIGHT:
Choose colour
and grade to
suit timber

least refined grade, and seldom used as a finish resin. 'Buttonlac' and 'garnet' are dark brown, 'orange' has a warm reddish tone and 'blond', 'lemon', or 'extra pale' are a light yellow. Bleached or 'white' shellac is treated in an alkali chlorine bath which makes it inherently unstable in liquid form. For this reason, I try to avoid this grade and use pale or lemon shellacs instead, which are filtered through activated charcoal.

Wax

Shellac contains between 3% to 5% wax, especially in orange and button grades, which is visible as a cloudy film which settles out when left to stand for a few days. This wax will make the dry shellac film less resistant to water-marking as well as reducing the gloss slightly. However, the wax can help to prevent the gumming of abrasive papers when power sanding, due to its lubricating action.

I prefer de-waxed grades such as 'extra pale', which is produced by filtering through active charcoal. De-waxed shellacs are harder, glossier and more water resistant, making them preferable for French polishing or for sealing under other finishes which will not tolerate wax.

"The secret of successful application lies in preparing shellac from dry flakes"

SPRAYING

Although this article is about hand finishes, many people never seem to think in terms of spraying shellac. This is a useful technique, in cases such as using a de-waxed shellac as a sealer under other finishes – manufacturers who warn again this are not critical of the shellac, so much as its wax content – always use de-waxed.

A 1½ to 2lb cut at about 30 PSI works well. It is not so different from spraying cellulose lacquer, but allow longer between coats as it dries more slowly – lacquer thinner is much more volatile than alcohol.

As with all spraying, test to refine the method so as to avoid an uneven 'orange-peel' surface – the pressure must be neither too low and the gun must not be held too far away. To avoid sags, drips or pin-holing the pressure must not be too high and the spraying must not be done too heavily, or too close to the surface.

Shellac reacts with steel, so aluminium airways in the gun are helpful. Clean the gun scrupulously with alcohol afterwards, although avoid prolonged soaking of the seals.

Spraying will be the slowest way to get a film build, but it can do things other methods can't – for example, airbrushes are invaluable in our restoration work for 'graining' and 'feathering in' on a repair.

If a full grain finish is required, avoid doing it all by spray, as the film structure is not as durable as that from a rubber or brush, which mechanically fuse the finish layers.

Preparation

The secret of successful application lies in preparing shellac from dry flakes. When mixed with alcohol, it begins to form chemical compounds called esters, which act as plasticisers to the dry film. Eventually, the liquid material will not dry at all. Even if liquid shellac has a date stamp on it when bought, the hapless purchaser has no idea if it has been stored properly – too high a temperature can drastically degrade shellac. Preparing your own gives you complete control over the quality.

I use either ordinary methylated spirits, clear IMS or reagent ethyl alcohol, which contains less water and is available from chemical suppliers.

I combine the flakes and alcohol in a non-metallic container. Liquid shellac is described in 'pound cuts' – a '3lb cut' refers to 3lbs of shellac to a gallon of alcohol. Proprietary liquid shellac is typically around a 3 to 4lb cut. I find a 1½ to 2lb cut is preferable for all uses. This is made by combining a pint of alcohol with ¼lb of shellac flakes. The exact ratios aren't critical – different shellac grades may require slightly more alcohol – but experimentation will produce the 'cut' you like.

> "Liquid shellac is described in 'pound cuts' – a '3lb cut' refers to 3lbs of shellac to a gallon of alcohol"

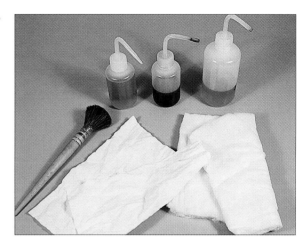

Mixing

This mixing process can be speeded up by crushing the flakes into a powder or standing the mix container in hot water – or doing both.

To produce a de-waxed shellac, allow the wax to settle and filter it off by straining it several times through cloth – or use pale de-waxed flakes.

By always using fresh shellac, you will greatly enhance the durability and water resistance of the dry film. I have tried to mark de-waxed shellac films with hot water for an hour or two without success – so much for the mythology!

Store liquid shellacs in a cool place and preferably keep them for no more than 3 to 4 months.

ABOVE: All the equipment you need – cotton and cotton wadding for the rubber, mop brush and useful bottles

LEFT: De-wax shellac by straining through a cloth several times

> "I have tried to mark de-waxed shellac films with hot water for an hour or two without success – so much for the mythology!"

OLD LIQUID

If old liquid shellac is found not to harden after application, you will have to strip it off and start again. Avoid the temptation to seal it in with fresh shellac – the top layer will soon start to crack. Apply a drop to a non-porous surface and if it hasn't dried hard after an hour or two, discard the remainder.

RIGHT: Fold the cotton outer covering around the wadding to produce a pointed 'egg' shape, and hold firmly as shown, to avoid juddering

SHELLAC GLOSS

Both brush and spray application offer another possibility – gloss is traditionally adjusted with abrasives on the completed surface. However, as with 'satin' varnishes, another way is to add flattening agents, such as fumed silica, to the resin. With shellac, this gives a softer degree of dullness, depending on the amount of flattening agent used, versus the somewhat brighter look of an abraded polished surface. This can be useful in toning repairs on old or antique surfaces.

It will not work with a rubber, as the wadding acts as a filter for the silica particles. Flattening agents are generally supplied for industrial use, but are also available for small scale finishing.

"Nitro-cellulose films will yellow and lose flexibility faster than shellac, increasing the chances of stress-cracking"

Other resins

Many 'French polish' suppliers add other resins such as nitro-cellulose to their liquid formulations; while these add a degree of water and alcohol resistance, in the longer term, they lack the chemical stability of shellac alone. Nitro-cellulose films will yellow and lose flexibility faster than shellac, increasing the chances of stress-cracking. This also applies to 'fadding lacquers', which, despite being sold as 'French polish', which is a technique not a material, contain substantial amounts of nitro-cellulose and resins other than shellac – the clue being in their solvent base, for example, methyl isobutyl ketone and ethyl acetate.

DAMAGE

Damage to shellac surfaces typically divides into two forms – heat damage and water marking. Heated objects and water will leave characteristic white markings on the surface. Water marking is more prevalent with higher wax content shellacs and is caused by moisture getting trapped in the film.

Careful application of alcohol with a fine pencil brush will re-dissolve the surface, allowing the moisture in the water marks to evaporate – or it can re-amalgamate the heat mark damage. This will disturb the surface texture and may require a rubber of shellac to level the marks. This works best with newer surfaces, say of 20 to 30 years, as even evaporative finishes will crosslink to some degree over time, becoming less soluble in the process.

Severe water and heat damage can mark the wood beneath, which typically produces a darker discolouration – this requires more involved remedial work.

These fadding lacquers also require a different application technique to traditional French polishing methods, and, to my eye, have a more 'plastic' appearance than shellac.

Application

Shellac can be applied by brush, spray or 'fadding', that is, French polishing. Needless to say, these methods can be combined – for example, initial coats of shellac can be sprayed or brushed, followed by a French polish rubber. In fact, this can be an invaluable time saver if there are large areas of woodwork to finish.

Fadding

While French polishing is often shrouded in craft lore and mystique, the principles are very simple. It is sometimes suggested that it is best to apply shellac with a rag alone – whilst this can work in simple applications, I find the traditional choice, of cotton wadding and a fine white cotton outer covering for the fad or rubber, is preferable.

The 'rubber' is merely a reservoir for the polish; however, other touted substitutes for wadding, such as cheesecloth, are not as good. The rubber releases the liquid shellac at just

the right rate without drips or whip marks. I won't go into an involved description of traditional French polish methods here – both the Sam Allen and Charles Hayward books are excellent for that, *see panel.*

The methodology is quite simple. Initially, shellac and alcohol are applied to the surface with the rubber; further applications of shellac and solvent soften the already deposited shellac and help to push it into the grain. The purpose of working in circles or figure-of-eights is primarily to fill the grain and prevent ridging, which can happen if the rubber is used solely with the grain.

Oil lubricants

It is often recommended to use a non-drying oil, such as raw linseed, as a lubricant. Having used both oil and not, I find its use greatly complicates the procedure and unquestionably damages the dried film.

Its main claim as a trade method is that it can allow a rapid build of polish – unfortunately trade methods serve a purpose which is at odds with the quality of the finish, namely repeat business! Let me clarify this point – any oil in the dry film will plasticise the

"The rubber releases the liquid shellac at just the right rate without drips or whip marks"

ABOVE: **Too much oil, or use of cellulose-reinforced fadding lacquers, can result in later cracking**

important; initially the rubber will move softened shellac around on the surface, blending new material with previous coats. Over time, gradually increase the amount of solvent (meths) applied to the outer cotton rubber face which lubricates by softening the deposited material.

Eventually, the rubber will be moving shellac about on the surface more than adding new material, and the process can be stopped to allow it to harden prior to flattening and applying the next coat.

With this somewhat wetter rubber, use a lighter touch to avoid putting too much shellac on the surface and producing whip marks. I have polished for hours like this, with no apparent sticking of the rubber. This approach means that there is no need for 'spiriting off', the film will not plasticise, and the whole process will be speeded up.

Otherwise the basic polishing procedures, including flattening and rubbing out with abrasives, can follow the orthodox methods.

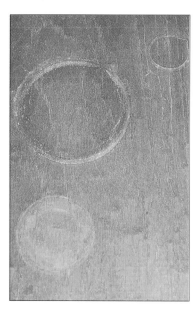

LEFT: **Typical water damage**

material and weaken it. Raw linseed oil will slowly polymerise by oxygen absorption and will expand in the process; shellac shrinks during the cure phase. This sets up a contradictory movement in the film structure, which is evidenced by the fine cracking seen in older shellac finishes. Linseed oil will also darken over time, degrading film clarity. Furthermore, the notion that the oil residues can be picked up by an alcohol laced rubber defies logic – oil is a hydrocarbon and is not soluble in polar solvents such as alcohol. Besides, the rubber is a reservoir, not a sponge!

Naphtha might be a better solvent choice, but this still assumes that all the oil rises magically to the surface during drying. However, the action of friction with the rubber during polishing ensures that, in reality, the oil is distributed throughout the film. This means that a 'spirit' rubber will merely soften the top surface and remove, at best, only a skim of oil with the shellac, leaving the majority in the film structure.

Control of rubber

Rather than using oil as a lubricant, proper control of the rubber should be developed – too slack a grip can cause juddering and sticking. Keeping an adequate supply of shellac in the rubber is

"I find that applying shellac with a rubber is the fastest way to achieve a finish build, as the fad actively pushes the resin into the pores"

TINTING

Shellacs are easily tinted with aniline 'spirit' dyes, such as with the trade 'red' and 'black' polish shellacs. Traditional base anilines tend to fade easily, but the metal-complex anilines, such as Orasol dyes, are much more lightfast, even in the volatile red/yellow spectrum. They are very concentrated, so one 4oz container in each colour will last the proverbial lifetime. They make shellacs an invaluable colour matching and shading medium. I generally use pale de-waxed shellac as the base, with the dye dissolved in alcohol first, before adding to the polish. Of course, different grades and colours of straight shellac can be mixed to produce varying colours too.

RIGHT: Typical heat damage

"The main trick is not to "back-brush" as with oil varnishes – this will tend to remove the material you have just laid down"

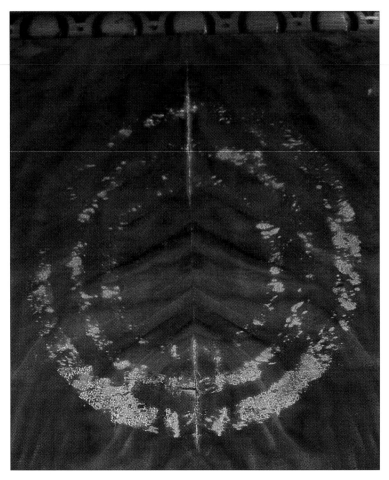

Oil as seal coat

If oil is used as a seal coat to enhance the grain definition, in place of 'fadding in' with shellac, make sure that polymerised boiled linseed is used. Apply it sparingly and allow sufficient time for it to cure before top coating with shellac – at least two days. This is to prevent a weakened bond between the polish film and the wood – sealing the oil with shellac too quickly will prevent oxygen from sufficiently curing the oil.

Lightly scuff sand the oil layer before applying the shellac over it.

Film cohesion

Applying shellac with a rubber allows thin coats of polish to be applied which are more stable and durable, in almost any film structure, than thick ones. The mechanical friction of the method also ensures excellent film cohesion, better than with a

"Sealing the oil with shellac too quickly will prevent oxygen from sufficiently curing the oil"

brush or spray. I find that applying shellac with a rubber is the fastest way to achieve a finish build, as the pad actively pushes the resin into the pores.

Brushing

Applying shellac by brush is straightforward. Use a good quality artists' grade brush, flat and reasonably soft, with either nylon or sable bristles – synthetic will last longer.

Again, keeping to a 1 to 2lb cut will ensure a film build generally free of ridging and streaking as can happen with heavier cuts. The main trick is not to 'back-brush' as with oil varnishes – this will tend to remove the material you have just laid down.

Cover the given area once entirely, then test with your finger to see when the coat is almost tack-free before applying another brush layer. Keep the brush reasonably loaded, but not so much that it drips.

Although the film build can seem slow, the object is not to create a thick coating. The fastest way to fill grain with finish is to sand between coats, rather than piling on more resin.

After eight or nine successive brush coats in a session, allow the surface to dry overnight. More shellac can be applied for a glossier finish, or the work rubbed out and waxed to finish the job. ■

"The fastest way to fill grain with finish is to sand between coats, rather than piling on more resin"

REFERENCE SOURCES

These articles are intended to be a primer rather than the sum of mankind's knowledge – further reading from the following bibliography is strongly recommended.

Understanding Wood Finishing
by Bob Flexner
Rodale Press, ISBN 0 87596 734 5

Staining and Polishing
by Charles Hayward
Out of print, sometimes available secondhand

Classic Finishing Techniques
by Sam Allen
Sterling, ISBN 0 8069 0513 1

Complete Manual of Wood Finishing
Frederick Oughton
Stobart Davies, ISBN 00 85442 030 4

Finishing off

Tim Judson gives the finishing touch to his series

ABOVE: Adding flattening agents, in the form of fumed silica, turns the finish opaque and lowers the gloss of the dry film

N THIS FINAL ARTICLE of the series we will be looking at hand-rubbing, as well as giving some thought to caring for finishes.

The object of hand-rubbing is to provide a silky-smooth, tactile surface, and a controlled level of gloss, reducing the hard glare of a newly-applied finish. It will also eliminate brush marks, rubber tracks, finish runs, orange peel and other defects. A variety of abrasives are used for this, some traditional and some relatively new compounds – but they all work towards this same end.

Hand-rubbing a finish is confined to those resins that are 'film-forming': shellac, oil varnish and polyurethanes, water-based finishes, and of course, the sprayed finishes like cellulose lacquer, conversion finishes and the like. Non film-forming finishes, such as oils, should not be rubbed because of the likelihood of sanding into bare wood – their smooth texture is a function of good pre-finish wood preparation.

RIGHT: Finish abrasive papers: silicone carbide, top left, Lubrisil paper, lower left, paper backed, top right, and heavier weight cloth backed, lower right

"Rubbing-out, which may sound more like a Mafia term, is the last crucial step needed to provide a high quality finish"

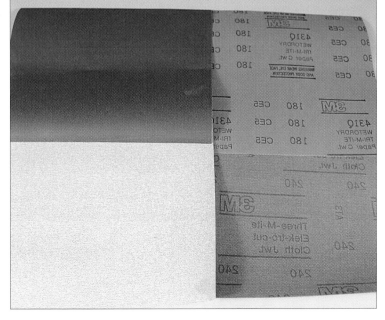

often skimped or omitted, yet it can spell the difference between a first-class job and a mediocre one. The reality is that the finish is usually the first thing that you notice on a piece of furniture – for better or worse!

Rubbing-out a finish involves firstly the removal of defects and then, either increasing the final gloss, or decreasing it to a flat or satin appearance. The choice of abrasives includes the following:
● abrasive paper, usually silicone carbide
● wire or steel wool, or synthetic steel wool pads
● rubbing compounds

"The finish is usually the first thing that you notice on a piece of furniture – for better or worse!"

Rubbing-out

Rubbing-out, which can sound more like a Mafia term, is the last crucial step needed to provide a high quality finish. No matter how carefully the finish is applied, there will always be a degree of imperfection in the dried finish surface from dust and other airborne contamination. The least affected of the film-forming finishes is a well-applied shellac French polish, as shellac cures quickly, and the rubber tends to level and clean the finish as it sweeps across it. The rubbing-out stage is too

Cure first

Before rubbing-out it is essential that the finish is allowed to fully cure out – abrading a still-soft finish will be a fruitless exercise and can cause considerable damage. A good rule is to allow a month to six weeks for any finish to cure out before rubbing. Evaporative finishes like shellac cure harder than reactive varnishes, making them easier to abrade.

Because this abrasive process will involve removal of some finish material, be sure to have

RUBBING MATERIALS

Rubbing materials include 0000 wire wool, powdered pumice and rottenstone abrasives, and automotive rubbing compounds.

The surface can be rubbed with wire wool to produce an even satin sheen; using paste wax as a lubricant with the wool will reduce its cutting action and raise the gloss somewhat. If a higher gloss is desired, pumice can be used with white spirit, or water on water-based finish, and a felt block or cloth. Rottenstone, available in various grades from F to FFFF which is the finest, can then be used to further refine the scratch pattern and raise the gloss. Both pumice and rottenstone can be bought pre-mixed or as a powder on its own. Premixed is usually supplied in oil, so I prefer to mix my own in solvent alone.

The finer grades of car finish rubbing compounds will give an even higher gloss, and can be used with a cloth pad or a powered buffing wheel. These are typically aluminium oxide particles in a solvent suspension. If a powered buffing wheel is used in place of a hand rubbing cloth, take care to keep it moving over the surface as it can generate significant heat and soften some finishes. Remove all residues of polishing compounds, as they can leave whitish deposits in cracks and pores. Remove these residues with water and a toothbrush and cover them with a dark paste wax polish.

"A hard proprietary paste wax, either plain or with a dark brown pigment, will produce excellent results"

Wax

Paste wax can be applied over flat surfaces with a chunk of wax wrapped in a cotton cloth pad, and wiped over the finish. The trick is to allow the solvent in the wax to evaporate until the wax starts to haze over, then burnish the excess wax off with a clean soft cloth. Because the solvent types can vary, this hazing can occur anywhere between 30 seconds and five minutes. The final wax film will increase the gloss and add some water resistance, but is not a protective film in its own right. Two applications are preferable to ensure full coverage – on carving or intricate work, a soft bristle brush can be used to apply wax sparingly as well as burnishing it off. If too much wax residue is visible, it can be wiped down with white spirit and burnished or re-waxed - the solvent in the new wax will soften the dry wax residues. Excess wax can cause smudges and will attract dirt.

Most proprietary waxes are blends of beeswax, carnauba, a very hard wax, paraffin and synthetic waxes. I see no great advantage in preparing your own, or in using beeswax alone, as the latter is too soft for the purpose. A hard proprietary paste wax, either plain or with a dark brown pigment, will produce excellent results.

enough clear top finish thickness to avoid sanding through layers of glaze, stain or toned finish. Layering, or sanding through to lower finish layers with visible 'witness' lines, can occur with varnishes and water-based finishes, particularly when they have been spray applied. The only remedy, if it occurs, is to apply more finish over the top, allow it to cure, and repeat the sanding process more carefully.

Removing defects

To remove surface blemishes, it will be necessary to level the finish with silicone carbide paper. This can either be used dry, generally in conjunction with a stearate lubricant, such as Lubrisil, to reduce sanding heat and to soften the finish, or wetted with liquid lubricants. Lubrisil is available up to about 800 grit and wet/dry to 2000 and up. Use a backing block on flat surfaces, or fingers in tighter areas and curves.

ABOVE: **Automotive buffing compounds, typically aluminium oxide particles in a suspension, can be used to produce high gloss finishes**

Liquid lubricants with wet/dry papers are either water, oil or white spirit. These liquids will all reduce corning, which is what occurs when the softened residues of the finish stick to the sandpaper. White spirit will give a fast cutting action, and will not react with any finishes except possibly some water-based ones – in which case switch to water lubricant. Mineral oil will virtually eliminate corning, while water, often with soap added, will still produce corning, but will cut quickly.

Initially finish levelling with wet/dry silicone carbide lubricated with water and soap

Gloss levels can be adjusted with pumice and rottenstone applied with white spirit and a cloth

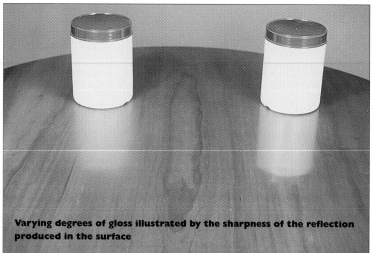

Varying degrees of gloss illustrated by the sharpness of the reflection produced in the surface

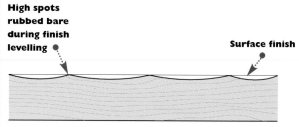

ABOVE: Fig I An uneven wood surface can produce bare spots during finish sanding

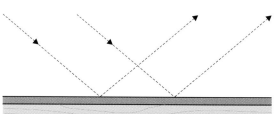

Light is evenly reflected from a smooth surface, increasing the appearance of gloss

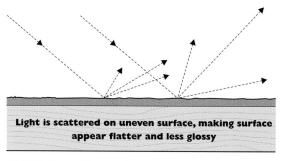

Light is scattered on uneven surface, making surface appear flatter and less glossy

ABOVE: Fig 2 Different light reflective characteristics of a finish surface

BELOW: Different waxes, clockwise from bottom left, pigmented dark wax, orange paste wax, hard pale wax, white synthetic microcrystalline wax

"Dried liquid lubricants can form opaque hazes and leave light coloured residues in wood pores"

If you sand through to bare wood, the water will raise the grain which can be hard to repair. This is liable to occur if the wood surface is uneven from tool or other surface markings, *see Fig 1*.

All these lubricants, especially mineral oil, will slow the cutting action while limiting corning. They can also be used with wire wool, 0000 grade, which tends to clog or corn much less than sandpaper.

ABOVE: A higher gloss, bottom, will also produce a darker apparent colour with greater grain definition

Progressive grits

At this stage it is still advisable to sand with the grain direction of the wood, as the abrasives involved are still relatively coarse. Progressively finer grits can be used, but remove sanding particles from the surface between each change. Take care on shaped components and edges where the film thickness is less – it is easy to sand through to bare wood.

Cleaning

If you plan to apply another layer of finish later, be sure to remove all abrasive and lubricant materials first. Steel wool particles can cause rust under water-based finishes, and soap or wax materials will not improve finish adhesion in any way! Thoroughly wash down with white spirit or naphtha, or water on water-base, before applying more finish. Otherwise, remove sanding residues carefully with a tack cloth or compressed air – dried liquid lubricants can form opaque hazes and leave light coloured residues in wood pores.

It is a good idea to use synthetic rather than wire wool pads on open-grained woods, especially oak, as residual metal particles can cause staining in the wood pores.

Final rubbing-out

The final rubbing-out is the process of adjusting the degree of gloss, after a uniformly smooth tactile surface has been achieved. Either wire wool or powdered abrasives are used to this end.

The degree of gloss is achieved by the amount of light which is scattered on the surface – large abrasive scratches will scatter light and lower the gloss level, while finer scratches will reflect light more evenly, increasing the overall sheen, *see Fig 2*. The gloss can also be adjusted by adding flatting agents – fumed silica – in the finish coats, which deflect light and produce flat or satin finishes. A good way to start is to apply a finish that is close to the appearance you want after rubbing.

Beyond that, either use coarser rubbing compounds to lower the gloss or progressively finer ones to increase it. Remember that adjusting the gloss will change the perceived colour – a higher gloss will make the wood appear darker and more translucent. It will also magnify any faults, so a low gloss is good in disguising unavoidable problems.

Concentration areas

You can use discretion when rubbing different finish areas – concentrate on horizontal topside surfaces which are highly visible. Table legs and chairs, and vertical surfaces in general, are less critical and will generally have less surface build anyway. 0000 wool with paste wax is often sufficient. By this stage, rubbing with the grain direction becomes less important as the abrasive grits and scratch patterns become progressively finer. ■

RIGHT: **One wax application method – place a ball of hard paste wax inside a cotton cloth**

BELOW RIGHT: **Applying the wax through the cloth controls the flow and prevents wax residues building in large wood pores, as on this oak mirror case**

"The final rubbing-out is the process of adjusting the degree of gloss, after a uniformly smooth tactile surface has been achieved"

CARING FOR FINISHES

Wood finishes benefit far more from passive care than active intervention. Passive care includes shielding the piece from exposure to strong sunlight as ultraviolet destroys the finish's molecular structure and discolours the wood. Keeping furniture away from excessive heat will slow natural oxidation processes which eventually cause finishes to crack and fail. Wood finishes can all be damaged by solvents, rough handling, water, and acids or alkalis, so treating them with a degree of restraint is the best form of protection. Table cloths and coasters are more beneficial than frequent waxings.

Active care

Active care includes periodic applications of wax, which can saturate the colour of the wood and provide a very limited degree of protection from water. Paste wax should be applied sparingly no more than once every six months.

Liquid or spray 'furniture polishes' are generally slow-evaporating hydrocarbon solvents which 'wet' the finish surface, but evaporate after a few days. They can solubilize grease marks but they often contain silicones and other additives which can harm the surface and complicate future re-finishings. The potential hazards of silicone are so bad that they should not be used in the workshop.

'Reviver' recipes based on meths, linseed oil, vinegar and such are also to be avoided at all costs – they represent the worst of the furniture restoration trade and do far more harm than good.

Finally, remember that there is a huge vested interest in getting people to buy 'furniture care' polishes and creams – the truth is that 'less is more' and passive care will be more beneficial overall. Wood finishes are often seriously damaged by indiscriminate cleaning methods – if you elect to have the work done by someone else, choose your restorer with care!

METRIC/IMPERIAL CONVERSION CHART

mm	inch	mm	inch	mm	inch	mm	inch
1	0.03937	26	1.02362	60	2.36220	310	12.20472
2	0.07874	27	1.06299	70	2.75590	320	12.59842
3	0.11811	28	1.10236	80	3.14960	330	12.99212
4	0.15748	29	1.14173	90	3.54330	340	13.38582
5	0.19685	30	1.18110	100	3.93700	350	13.77952
6	0.23622	31	1.22047	110	4.33070	360	14.17322
7	0.27559	32	1.25984	120	4.72440	370	14.56692
8	0.31496	33	1.29921	130	5.11811	380	14.96063
9	0.35433	34	1.33858	140	5.51181	390	15.35433
10	0.39370	35	1.37795	150	5.90551	400	15.74803
11	0.43307	36	1.41732	160	6.29921	410	16.14173
12	0.47244	37	1.45669	170	6.69291	420	16.53543
13	0.51181	38	1.49606	180	7.08661	430	16.92913
14	0.55118	39	1.53543	190	7.48031	440	17.32283
15	0.59055	40	1.57480	200	7.87401	450	17.71653
16	0.62992	41	1.61417	210	8.26771	460	18.11023
17	0.66929	42	1.65354	220	8.66141	470	18.50393
18	0.70866	43	1.69291	230	9.05511	480	18.89763
19	0.74803	44	1.73228	240	9.44881	490	19.29133
20	0.78740	45	1.77165	250	9.84252	500	19.68504
21	0.82677	46	1.81102	260	10.23622		
22	0.86614	47	1.85039	270	10.62992		
23	0.90551	48	1.88976	280	11.02362		
24	0.94488	49	1.92913	290	11.41732		
25	0.98425	50	1.96850	300	11.81102		

1 mm = 0.03937 inch
1 cm = 0.3937 inch
1 m = 3.281 feet
1 inch = 25.4 mm
1 foot = 304.8 mm
1 yard = 914.4 mm

IMPERIAL/METRIC CONVERSION CHART

inch		mm	inch		mm	inch		mm
0	0	0	23/64	0.359375	9.1281	45/64	0.703125	17.8594
1/64	0.015625	0.3969				23/32	0.71875	18.2562
1/32	0.03125	0.7938	3/8	0.375	9.5250	47/64	0.734375	18.6531
3/64	0.046875	1.1906	25/64	0.390625	9.9219			
1/16	0.0625	1.5875	13/32	0.40625	10.3188	3/4	0.750	19.0500
			27/64	0.421875	10.7156			
5/64	0.078125	1.9844				49/64	0.765625	19.4469
3/32	0.09375	2.3812	7/16	0.4375	11.1125	25/32	0.78125	19.8438
7/64	0.109375	2.7781	29/64	0.453125	11.5094	51/64	0.796875	20.2406
			15/32	0.46875	11.9062	13/16	0.8125	20.6375
1/8	0.125	3.1750	31/64	0.484375	12.3031			
9/64	0.140625	3.5719				53/64	0.828125	21.0344
5/32	0.15625	3.9688	1/2	0.500	12.700	27/32	0.84375	21.4312
11/64	0.171875	4.3656	33/64	0.515625	13.0969	55/64	0.858375	21.8281
			17/32	0.53125	13.4938			
3/16	0.1875	4.7625	35/64	0.546875	13.8906	7/8	0.875	22.2250
13/64	0.203125	5.1594	9/16	0.5625	14.2875	57/64	0.890625	22.6219
7/32	0.21875	5.5562				29/32	0.90625	23.0188
15/64	0.234375	5.9531	37/64	0.578125	14.6844	59/64	0.921875	23.4156
1/4	0.250	6.3500	19/32	0.59375	15.0812			
			39/64	0.609375	15.4781	15/16	0.9375	23.8125
17/64	0.265625	6.7469				61/64	0.953125	24.2094
9/32	0.28125	7.1438	5/8	0.625	15.8750	31/32	0.96875	24.6062
19/64	0.296875	7.5406	41/64	0.640625	16.2719	63/64	0.984375	25.0031
5/16	0.3125	7.9375	21/32	0.65625	16.6688			
			43/64	0.671875	17.0656			
21/64	0.1328125	8.3344						
11/32	0.34375	8.7312	11/16	0.6875	17.4625	1 inch = 1.000 = 25.40 mm		

INDEX

TITLES AVAILABLE FROM
GMC Publications
BOOKS

WOODCARVING

The Art of the Woodcarver	*GMC Publications*
Carving Architectural Detail in Wood: The Classical Tradition	
	Frederick Wilbur
Carving Birds & Beasts	*GMC Publications*
Carving Nature: Wildlife Studies in Wood	*Frank Fox-Wilson*
Carving Realistic Birds	*David Tippey*
Decorative Woodcarving	*Jeremy Williams*
Elements of Woodcarving	*Chris Pye*
Essential Tips for Woodcarvers	*GMC Publications*
Essential Woodcarving Techniques	*Dick Onians*
Further Useful Tips for Woodcarvers	*GMC Publications*
Lettercarving in Wood: A Practical Course	*Chris Pye*
Making & Using Working Drawings for Realistic Model Animals	
	Basil F. Fordham

Power Tools for Woodcarving	*David Tippey*
Practical Tips for Turners & Carvers	*GMC Publications*
Relief Carving in Wood: A Practical Introduction	*Chris Pye*
Understanding Woodcarving	*GMC Publications*
Understanding Woodcarving in the Round	*GMC Publications*
Useful Techniques for Woodcarvers	*GMC Publications*
Wildfowl Carving – Volume 1	*Jim Pearce*
Wildfowl Carving – Volume 2	*Jim Pearce*
Woodcarving: A Complete Course	*Ron Butterfield*
Woodcarving: A Foundation Course	*Zoë Gertner*
Woodcarving for Beginners	*GMC Publications*
Woodcarving Tools & Equipment Test Reports	*GMC Publications*
Woodcarving Tools, Materials & Equipment	*Chris Pye*

WOODTURNING

Adventures in Woodturning	*David Springett*
Bert Marsh: Woodturner	*Bert Marsh*
Bowl Turning Techniques Masterclass	*Tony Boase*
Colouring Techniques for Woodturners	*Jan Sanders*
Contemporary Turned Wood: New Perspectives in a Rich Tradition	
	Ray Leier, Jan Peters & Kevin Wallace
The Craftsman Woodturner	*Peter Child*
Decorative Techniques for Woodturners	*Hilary Bowen*
Fun at the Lathe	*R.C. Bell*
Further Useful Tips for Woodturners	*GMC Publications*
Illustrated Woodturning Techniques	*John Hunnex*
Intermediate Woodturning Projects	*GMC Publications*
Keith Rowley's Woodturning Projects	*Keith Rowley*
Practical Tips for Turners & Carvers	*GMC Publications*
Turning Green Wood	*Michael O'Donnell*
Turning Miniatures in Wood	*John Sainsbury*

Turning Pens and Pencils	*Kip Christensen & Rex Burningham*
Understanding Woodturning	*Ann & Bob Phillips*
Useful Techniques for Woodturners	*GMC Publications*
Useful Woodturning Projects	*GMC Publications*
Woodturning: Bowls, Platters, Hollow Forms, Vases,	
Vessels, Bottles, Flasks, Tankards, Plates	*GMC Publications*
Woodturning: A Foundation Course (New Edition)	*Keith Rowley*
Woodturning: A Fresh Approach	*Robert Chapman*
Woodturning: An Individual Approach	*Dave Regester*
Woodturning: A Source Book of Shapes	*John Hunnex*
Woodturning Jewellery	*Hilary Bowen*
Woodturning Masterclass	*Tony Boase*
Woodturning Techniques	*GMC Publications*
Woodturning Tools & Equipment Test Reports	*GMC Publications*
Woodturning Wizardry	*David Springett*

WOODWORKING

Bird Boxes and Feeders for the Garden	*Dave Mackenzie*
Complete Woodfinishing	*Ian Hosker*
David Charlesworth's Furniture-Making Techniques	
	David Charlesworth
Furniture & Cabinetmaking Projects	*GMC Publications*
Furniture-Making Projects for the Wood Craftsman	*GMC Publications*
Furniture-Making Techniques for the Wood Craftsman	*GMC Publications*
Furniture Projects	*Rod Wales*
Furniture Restoration (Practical Crafts)	*Kevin Jan Bonner*
Furniture Restoration and Repair for Beginners	*Kevin Jan Bonner*
Furniture Restoration Workshop	*Kevin Jan Bonner*
Green Woodwork	*Mike Abbott*
Kevin Ley's Furniture Projects	*Kevin Ley*
Making & Modifying Woodworking Tools	*Jim Kingshott*
Making Chairs and Tables	*GMC Publications*
Making Classic English Furniture	*Paul Richardson*
Making Little Boxes from Wood	*John Bennett*
Making Shaker Furniture	*Barry Jackson*
Making Woodwork Aids and Devices	*Robert Wearing*
Minidrill: Fifteen Projects	*John Everett*

Pine Furniture Projects for the Home	*Dave Mackenzie*
Practical Scrollsaw Patterns	*John Everett*
Router Magic: Jigs, Fixtures and Tricks to	
Unleash your Router's Full Potential	*Bill Hylton*
Routing for Beginners	*Anthony Bailey*
The Scrollsaw: Twenty Projects	*John Everett*
Sharpening: The Complete Guide	*Jim Kingshott*
Sharpening Pocket Reference Book	*Jim Kingshott*
Simple Scrollsaw Projects	*GMC Publications*
Space-Saving Furniture Projects	*Dave Mackenzie*
Stickmaking: A Complete Course	*Andrew Jones & Clive George*
Stickmaking Handbook	*Andrew Jones & Clive George*
Test Reports: *The Router* and *Furniture & Cabinetmaking*	
	GMC Publications
Veneering: A Complete Course	*Ian Hosker*
Woodfinishing Handbook (Practical Crafts)	*Ian Hosker*
Woodworking with the Router: Professional	
Router Techniques any Woodworker can Use	
	Bill Hylton & Fred Matlack
The Workshop	*Jim Kingshott*

UPHOLSTERY

The Upholsterer's Pocket Reference Book	*David James*
Upholstery: A Complete Course (Revised Edition)	*David James*
Upholstery Restoration	*David James*

Upholstery Techniques & Projects	*David James*
Upholstery Tips and Hints	*David James*

TOYMAKING

Designing & Making Wooden Toys	*Terry Kelly*
Fun to Make Wooden Toys & Games	*Jeff & Jennie Loader*
Restoring Rocking Horses	*Clive Green & Anthony Dew*

Scrollsaw Toy Projects	*Ivor Carlyle*
Scrollsaw Toys for All Ages	*Ivor Carlyle*
Wooden Toy Projects	*GMC Publications*

DOLLS' HOUSES AND MINIATURES

Architecture for Dolls' Houses	*Joyce Percival*
A Beginners' Guide to the Dolls' House Hobby	*Jean Nisbett*
Celtic, Medieval and Tudor Wall Hangings in 1/12 Scale Needlepoint	
	Sandra Whitehead
The Complete Dolls' House Book	*Jean Nisbett*
The Dolls' House 1/24 Scale: A Complete Introduction	*Jean Nisbett*
Dolls' House Accessories, Fixtures and Fittings	*Andrea Barham*
Dolls' House Bathrooms: Lots of Little Loos	*Patricia King*
Dolls' House Fireplaces and Stoves	*Patricia King*
Easy to Make Dolls' House Accessories	*Andrea Barham*
Heraldic Miniature Knights	*Peter Greenhill*
How to Make Your Dolls' House Special: Fresh Ideas for Decorating	
	Beryl Armstrong
Make Your Own Dolls' House Furniture	*Maurice Harper*
Making Dolls' House Furniture	*Patricia King*

Making Georgian Dolls' Houses	*Derek Rowbottom*
Making Miniature Gardens	*Freida Gray*
Making Miniature Oriental Rugs & Carpets	*Meik & Ian McNaughton*
Making Period Dolls' House Accessories	*Andrea Barham*
Making 1/12 Scale Character Figures	*James Carrington*
Making Tudor Dolls' Houses	*Derek Rowbottom*
Making Victorian Dolls' House Furniture	*Patricia King*
Miniature Bobbin Lace	*Roz Snowden*
Miniature Embroidery for the Georgian Dolls' House	*Pamela Warner*
Miniature Embroidery for the Victorian Dolls' House	*Pamela Warner*
Miniature Needlepoint Carpets	*Janet Granger*
More Miniature Oriental Rugs & Carpets	*Meik & Ian McNaughton*
Needlepoint 1/12 Scale: Design Collections for the Dolls' House	
	Felicity Price
The Secrets of the Dolls' House Makers	*Jean Nisbett*

CRAFTS

American Patchwork Designs in Needlepoint	*Melanie Tacon*
A Beginners' Guide to Rubber Stamping	*Brenda Hunt*
Blackwork: A New Approach	*Brenda Day*
Celtic Cross Stitch Designs	*Carol Phillipson*
Celtic Knotwork Designs	*Sheila Sturrock*
Celtic Knotwork Handbook	*Sheila Sturrock*
Celtic Spirals and Other Designs	*Sheila Sturrock*
Collage from Seeds, Leaves and Flowers	*Joan Carver*
Complete Pyrography	*Stephen Poole*
Contemporary Smocking	*Dorothea Hall*
Creating Colour with Dylon	*Dylon International*
Creative Doughcraft	*Patricia Hughes*
Creative Embroidery Techniques Using Colour Through Gold	
	Daphne J. Ashby & Jackie Woolsey
The Creative Quilter: Techniques and Projects	*Pauline Brown*
Decorative Beaded Purses	*Enid Taylor*
Designing and Making Cards	*Glennis Gilruth*
Glass Engraving Pattern Book	*John Everett*
Glass Painting	*Emma Sedman*
How to Arrange Flowers: A Japanese Approach to English Design	
	Taeko Marvelly
An Introduction to Crewel Embroidery	*Mave Glenny*
Making and Using Working Drawings for Realistic Model Animals	
	Basil F. Fordham
Making Character Bears	*Valerie Tyler*

Making Decorative Screens	*Amanda Howes*
Making Fairies and Fantastical Creatures	*Julie Sharp*
Making Greetings Cards for Beginners	*Pat Sutherland*
Making Hand-Sewn Boxes: Techniques and Projects	*Jackie Woolsey*
Making Knitwear Fit	*Pat Ashforth & Steve Plummer*
Making Mini Cards, Gift Tags & Invitations	*Glennis Gilruth*
Making Soft-Bodied Dough Characters	*Patricia Hughes*
Natural Ideas for Christmas: Fantastic Decorations to Make	
	Josie Cameron-Ashcroft & Carol Cox
Needlepoint: A Foundation Course	*Sandra Hardy*
Patchwork for Beginners	*Pauline Brown*
Pyrography Designs	*Norma Gregory*
Pyrography Handbook (Practical Crafts)	*Stephen Poole*
Ribbons and Roses	*Lee Lockheed*
Rose Windows for Quilters	*Angela Besley*
Rubber Stamping with Other Crafts	*Lynne Garner*
Sponge Painting	*Ann Rooney*
Step-by-Step Pyrography Projects for the Solid Point Machine	
	Norma Gregory
Tassel Making for Beginners	*Enid Taylor*
Tatting Collage	*Lindsay Rogers*
Temari: A Traditional Japanese Embroidery Technique	*Margaret Ludlow*
Theatre Models in Paper and Card	*Robert Burgess*
Wool Embroidery and Design	*Lee Lockheed*

VIDEOS

Drop-in and Pinstuffed Seats	*David James*
Stuffover Upholstery	*David James*
Elliptical Turning	*David Springett*
Woodturning Wizardry	*David Springett*
Turning Between Centres: The Basics	*Dennis White*
Turning Bowls	*Dennis White*
Boxes, Goblets and Screw Threads	*Dennis White*
Novelties and Projects	*Dennis White*
Classic Profiles	*Dennis White*

Twists and Advanced Turning	*Dennis White*
Sharpening the Professional Way	*Jim Kingshott*
Sharpening Turning & Carving Tools	*Jim Kingshott*
Bowl Turning	*John Jordan*
Hollow Turning	*John Jordan*
Woodturning: A Foundation Course	*Keith Rowley*
Carving a Figure: The Female Form	*Ray Gonzalez*
The Router: A Beginner's Guide	*Alan Goodsell*
The Scroll Saw: A Beginner's Guide	*John Burke*

MAGAZINES

WOODTURNING ◆ WOODCARVING ◆ FURNITURE & CABINETMAKING
THE ROUTER ◆ WOODWORKING ◆ THE DOLLS' HOUSE MAGAZINE
WATER GARDENING ◆ EXOTIC GARDENING ◆ GARDEN CALENDAR
OUTDOOR PHOTOGRAPHY ◆ BUSINESSMATTERS

The above represents a selection of all titles currently published or scheduled to be published.
All are available direct from the Publishers or through bookshops, newsagents and specialist retailers.
To place an order, or to obtain a complete catalogue, contact:

GMC Publications,
Castle Place, 166 High Street, Lewes, East Sussex BN7 1XU, United Kingdom
Tel: 01273 488005 Fax: 01273 478606
E-mail: pubs@thegmcgroup.com

Orders by credit card are accepted